AF227827

for Laurie,

Jordan, Paige, Alex & Imogen

ABOUT ROOKWOOD STUDIOS

Rookwood Studios is a converted farm courtyard on the coast in West Wales and is home to The Natural Gallery and Habitat Info. The former is a gallery dedicated to promoting a celebration of wildlife art and related publications. Habitat Info is a GIS lab (Geographic Information Systems) where mapping technologies are applied to help people adapt to the harmful effects of climate change and to help wildlife survive the loss of their liveable habitats. Our home at Llanunwas, Solva is a 25 acre farm falling between the St Davids Coastal Special Area of Conservation and the the North Pembrokeshire commons SAC. We work with Rob's brothers Chris and Andy, our farm tenants and our neighbours The Bug Farm to restore natural habitats and lost species to the area and to rehabilitate injured wildlife. Habitat Info developed a mobile app with The Peregrine Fund for recording surveys of raptors which we used in this publication for logging our route and sightings (freely available at www.globalraptors.org) and provides other technical expertise to support various databases local and global. www.rookwoodstudios.com

HOW YOU CAN HELP VULTURES THROUGH THIS BOOK

Vultures were a predominant species that we encountered on our journey because they are doing pretty well in Spain and especially in the savanna habitats. But this has not always been the case and today vultures are declining at an alarming rate around the world especially in Africa where some of the Griffon Vultures migrate to from Spain during the northern winter. The declines are mainly driven by the ease with which an entire colony of vultures may be wiped out with a single careless poisoning event which are often not even directed at vultures. In India nearly all the vultures were extinguished by an anti-inflammatory drug used on cattle (diclofenac), and the consequences of losing these important scavengers have been devastating to the local ecology and economy: the increased incidence of diseases (rabies and anthrax) are thought to have cost the Indian government about $1.5bn annually during the absence of vultures. But bird of prey populations can recover when the threats are removed and Spain has been a success story for vultures with Griffon Vultures increasing from 5000 to 30000 pairs. And we must have seen a sizeable portion of these pairs on the mountain tops that we passed on our journey for this book. Cork Oak savanna is clearly a vital habitat enabling vultures to forage and survive in modern Europe so we will be very glad to direct 10% of net proceeds from sales of this collection of paintings, the book, prints and maps to the Vulture Conservation Foundation which operates efficiently for the conservation of these birds in Europe. You can read more about this on pages 40-43 and we will direct 25% of net proceeds from the sale of the Griffon Vulture plate on page 43.

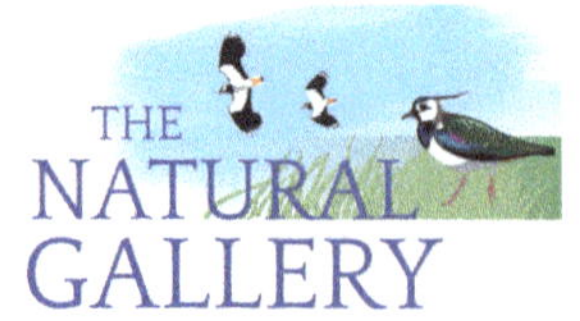
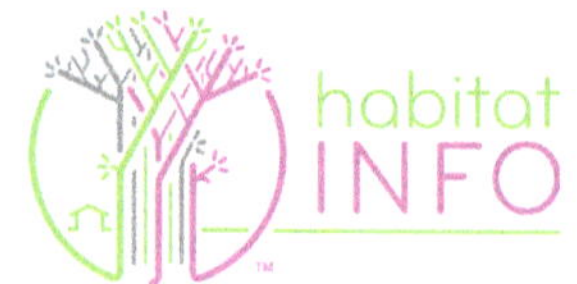
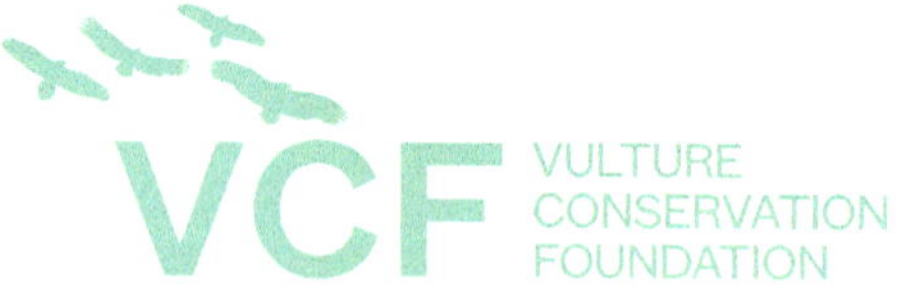

Our Journey through the Cork Oaks

around the savanna habitats of Portugal and Spain in 30 days

Rob Davies & Amanda Squire

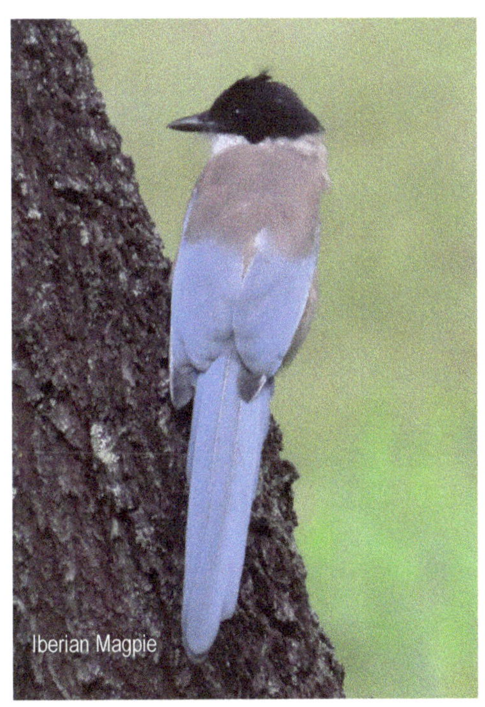

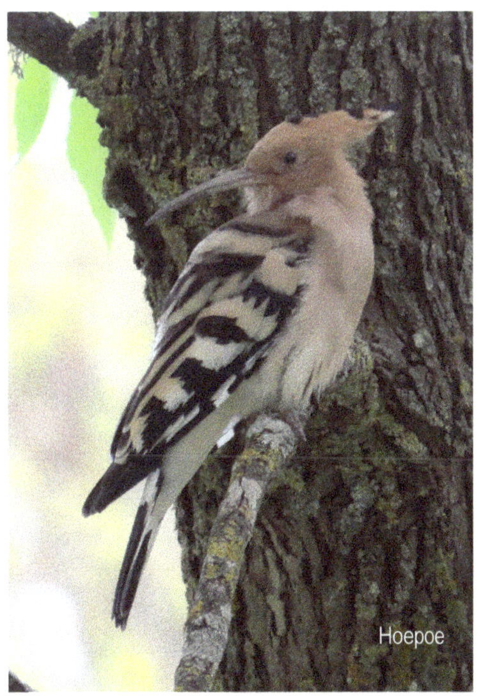

a catalogue of artworks and anecdotes

Copyright © 2024 by Rob Davies & Amanda Squire. All rights reserved

This book or any portion thereof may not be reproduced or used in any manner whatsoever without the express written permission of the publisher except for the use of brief quotations in a book review

Strenuous attempts have been made to credit all copyrighted materials used in this book. All such materials and trademarks, which are referenced in this book, are the full property of their respective copyright owners. Every effort has been made to obtain permission for material quoted in this book. Any omissions will be rectified in future editions.

Editing & Design: Rookwood Studios

Printed in the United Kingdom

First Printing, 2024

ISBN: 978-1-7385439-1-5 (Paperback)

ISBN: 978-1-7385439-0-8 (eBook)

Rookwood Studios

Llanunwas, Solva, Pembrokeshire

SA62 6UJ

www.rookwoodstudios.com

TABLE OF CONTENTS

ACKNOWLEDGMENTS

We would like to thank Rob's brother Mark for convening an amazing gathering on the event of his 60th birthday party in Lisbon and giving us this good reason to make our journey South in Myfanwy.

Our great friend Paddy Waller meticulously researched travel logistics and things to see and do around the Sierra de San Pedro and the Sierra Gredos, and helped us appreciate all things Spanish and Portuguese especially the food and wine and trekking.

Simon and Lulu Williams helped us plan our van route through northern Spain and found some wonderful places to stop and enjoy.

We would like to thank Simon Trice, Mandy Fish, Ffion Rees and Laurie for holding the fort at Rookwood and the Hawk Hotel while we were away, and looking after the menagerie.

The mobile mapping app used in our travels to log sightings and our route is freely provided by The Peregrine Fund's GRIN project (www.globalraptors.org) and facilitated by inclusion of this project in the ESRI environment grant programme. ESRI have generously helped with mapping software throughout Rob's conservation work, and Simon Trice assisted to use ArcMap to produce the map of our journey on page 8 and 9.

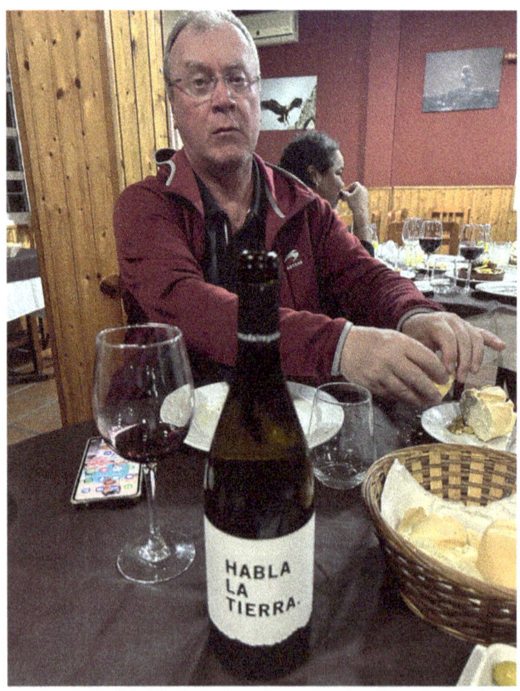

Paddy Waller educating us on local food and wines

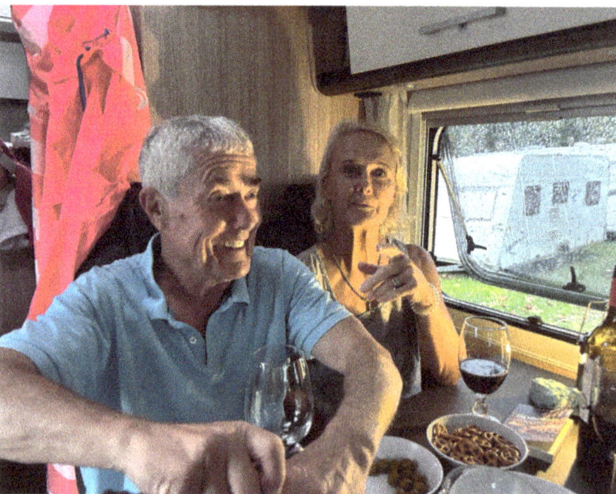

Simon and Lulu Williams enjoying the van life

PREFACE

Certainly as a landscape artist or photographer and probably as a human it is possible to fall in love with a landscape, to believe in a place.

We have been in love with Pembrokeshire for a long while now: the freedom of the cliffs and the wild sea, the blazes of gorse and wind-sculpted tree forms, and the overlooking grey dolerite inselbergs of Carn Llydi and Penberi – all add great character to the land. Our friend Ros Evans who paints the colours and emotions of Pembrokeshire speaks of the light effects, moods and atmospheres where land meets sea and where sea meets sky.

Africa stretched horizons further for one of us. Rob spent his first two decades as an adult in the arid interiors of South Africa in the Karoo and he truly learned great space and big skies when he arrived there: with roads that led for 30 miles without a hint of any change of direction, traversing massive expansive flat plains with snaking rivers, and similar dolerite inselbergs and escarpments overlooking these though more geometric in their intricate erosion patterns, a place so desolately beautiful it made you weep when you arrived and made you weep when you left.

Next to the Karoo and across miles and miles of bloody Africa stretches the Kalahari, not a desert as it is commonly thought of, but an arid savanna receiving just enough rain that beautiful thorn trees can grow but not so much rain that the trees grow large and converge into a closed forest. Savanna(h) is a great word describing this habitat of spaced trees allowing a ground cover of grasses and herbs to flourish when the rains allow and where wildfire may be a regular event. Savanna is one of the richest wildlife habitats and home to the phenomenon of Africa's 'big game' – Daktari- and safari- land. The spacing of the trees is crucial to the lives of many species particularly the hunters: big cats and big birds of prey. The enormous eagles and vultures found here need open space to land on their prey or carcases, and they need runway areas to take off again with their cargo of meat. In Africa the phenomenon of bush encroachment can actually render vast areas of habitat inaccessible to vultures because there is not enough take-off space.

So it was with great joy that we discovered a savanna habitat does exist in Europe in fact the word comes from the Spanish word *sabanna* which itself was brought from the Carribean *zabanna* a Taino Native American word meaning treeless plain. From a bird's eye view today's savannas are predominantly grass or bare earth but they are dotted with trees. Two trees dominate the savannas of Spain, Portugal and North Africa, the Holm Oak and the Cork Oak. Cork Oaks are uniquely adapted with their thick soft bark to survive regular fires and can actually sprout buds directly from their burnt branches. In many ways the Cork Oak savannas reminds us of the beautiful savannas of Africa. Both are hard arid lands but show in the softest pastel colours and in the strong sunlight the sweeping grey Cork Oaks could be mistaken for the Camelthorns of the Kalahari. The shade beneath these trees is obviously important to animals and plants living in these hot environments and Rob was amazed to see the same bright green undergrowth sprouting after rains in this microclimate enriched by the rain of seed pods / acorns and leaves from above.

Our artist friend Paul MacDermot accompanied Rob on a painting safari through the Kalahari and commented that from a colour and tone point of view these are more simple landscapes. Certainly they lack the complexity of greens of our British landscape and are a relief for mixing colours!

But these arid savannas are indeed more simple in a biological way. We don't mean they lack diversity, quite the contrary, they boast fantastic biodiversity. Cork Oak Savanna has been found to support up to 135 species of vascular plants within a tenth of a hectare. But all the animals and plants in this landscape are bound by a single most important survival task – to endure hot dry conditions. Even the baby leaves of these oaks emerge holly-like as tiny tough spikey versions of an oak leaf, their own version of thorns to survive herbivores and droughts. This has always appealed to Rob's curiosity for biology. It is possible to understand the ecological workings of these arid landscapes in a way which is elusive for more humid environments. Everything is held in check until the rains come and there are some amazing adaptations for living without water.

In rocky terrain and on mounds these dryland oak trees grow out of the ground at improbable angles (just like the Ghwarrieboom trees of the Eastern Cape Karoo) so their canopies capture the sun and these shape-full, dotted skylines add great character to the colourful landscape like the wind-blown tree forms of Pembrokeshire.

Cork Oak Savannas have been recognised for their biological importance and feature for protection under the European Union's Habitats Directive. But this protection has been tardy and a few decades ago conservationists were very concerned about the status of the dehesas in Spain and the montados in Portugal. There is a pragmatic saying in conservation in Africa, if it pays it stays. And people have known for centuries that Cork Oaks do pay – both in the cutting away of the thick buoyant bark revealing bare sangria coloured trunks every nine years or so, for use as fishing floats, corks for wine bottles, dart boards and even the nose cones of spaceships; and also in the fall of acorns onto the ground beneath which has fed generations of pigs for their Iberian *Jamón*, or the wild boars and deer pursued by the hunters. It is this value of the trees that has secured better protection in recent decades with more funding to manage the landscapes. Cork Oak forests are mainly privately owned and these are defended with rigorous security of barbed wire fences and heavily chained metal farm gates. We actually found it a frustration on our journey through miles and miles of fabulous habitat on good but narrow roads where it was impossible to pull off and stop and soak in the sounds and sights of it all. The word dehesa translates as private. However this inaccessibility to large parts of Cork Oak savannas is a price worth paying for the preservation of the rare wildlife habitat within. In North Africa these forests are communally owned and, with the tragedy of the commons, they are over-used and not sustained.

There was one type of site that we could always find somewhere to stop and enjoy the oaks and the scenery – these are the dolmen sites or standing stones which identify the rich archaeological and cultural history of the landscape. These are usually well signed from the road and you can usually wind your way along remote rocky tracks to somewhere very special. There is little doubt that the people living at these sites all those thousands of years ago found them equally or more special than we did. Some of them offer up incredible vistas overlooking giant valleys from lookouts where hunter-gatherer communities could have been in constant visual contact with the landscape and resources that they depended on.

The dolmens of Spain must have been of great spiritual significance to the Neolithic inhabitants just as the standing stone sites were for the ancient people of Pembrokeshire and just as the rock art murals were for the Bushmen of the Karoo. All of these peoples would have moved a lot, maybe seasonally to cope with changes in rainfall and food so perhaps these sites also served as markers too – that there are people living here. Rob was amazed to learn in the Karoo that the Bushmen inhabited this land thousands of years before at the same densities (1-2 persons per km2) as the current inhabitants on modern ranches. Whether it is St David's purple sandstone cathedral nestled in under Carn Llydi, attracting the pilgrims, or the blue stone burial chamber at Pentre Ifan visible from Cardigan Bay, and the Dolmen sites in Spain, all of these ancient sites mark places to believe in no matter your religion.

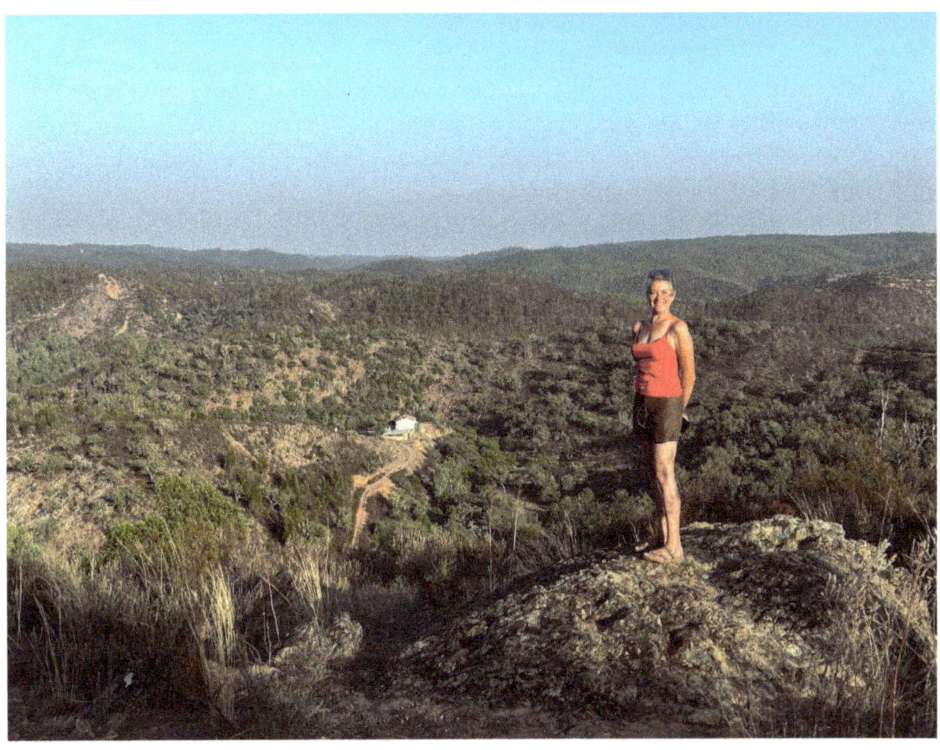

Amanda at a dolmen site North of Aracena

INTRODUCTION

For Rob, as a very young teenager, a family holiday to Fuengirola South of Malaga in 1972 was an eye-opener. For the first time he could explore a truly wild landscape in the mountains or sierra above the town.

Rob recounts his experiences of Spain..

"I was so excited to see my first big birds of prey in the skies, not really knowing what they were then, and fascinated at the craggy conifers growing directly out of hard rock; but equally shocked to see shotgun cartridges littering the ground almost everywhere. I found a small zoo in town and there at the end of the cages sat a sad row of injured hawks, falcons and eagles. It was the Hobby that caught my emotion I had never seen one before, such a beautiful fragile falcon, and its name in Spanish has been with me since that day, it was simply labelled: *El Alcotan*.

Things have been turned around since then in Spain, followed by Italy and other Mediterranean states. Thanks to the hard work of conservationists the mad craze to shoot anything that flies has largely passed over in these countries while we still wait for Malta and Lebanon and other to come to their senses. I joined some of these conservationists from Fundacion Migres to watch the raptor migration into Spain at Tarifa, and in a single day 16/4/2011 we counted over 1000 Booted Eagles returning from their northern winter in Africa.

Since coming back from working in conservation in Africa in 2001 I have also been very lucky to join my great friend Paddy Waller who began a tradition of taking his three sons and friends up a different mountain range in Spain every year if possible. Spain is the most mountainous country in Europe after Switzerland so there has been no shortage of these. I went on three of these amazing trekking holidays. Paddy married a wonderful Spanish lady Julia and settled in Xativa where for a while they ran a culinary and culture holiday company as well as imports of food and wine from Spain into UK. So the treks were long and hard but always wonderful food and wine and a comfy bed as a reward! While dodging the wild bulls we met in these spectacular landscapes and with the amazing raptors and wildlife to watch on these trips I think it's fair to say Spain was giving me my Africa fix, as much as possible, in Europe!

There is another similarity between Spain and Africa which is that Spain, along with Portugal, holds the largest expanse of a savanna habitat in Europe. It is the Cork Oak and Holm Oak savanna known as *Dehesa* in Spain and *Montado* in Portugal. I first read about the Dehesa while in Africa and became fascinated that such a habitat could still exist in the middle of developed Europe, with vulture, eagles, wild boars and predators. I set a bucket-list item to get there one day.

In September 2023 my partner, Amanda Squire, and I were able to make this experience happen at last. We completed the conversion of our trusty van (affectionately know to us as Myfanwy) with an upstairs extension for sleeping and various painting adaptations including the installation of a rather out of place office chair, and we set off by ferry from Fishguard to Rosslare in Ireland and then down to Bilbao. And so, our five-week and 4000 mile adventure to Extremadura in Spain and to Alentejo in Portugal began.

For Amanda it was a badly needed holiday and a chance to develop photography with her favourite subjects in a new setting. For Rob it was a chance to get back into painting and sketching of wildlife and to get to know the colours of another wild arid landscape. And for both of us it was a bit of van life and meeting up with good friends. By great coincidence my good friend Lulu Williams from university days and her husband Simon were doing a similar van holiday mainly in northern Spain so we began with a couple of very relaxing days by the beach with them. We then had to get to my brother Mark's 60th birthday party in Lisbon, a fancy-dress 3-day extravaganza with friends and family. It was quite a trek to get there in two days so we put foot and didn't stop much those first few days. Our main trip to the savannas began 10 September as we headed east from Lisbon into Alentejo province. Paddy joined us for a week to explore Extremadura and do a bit of hiking. It was great to share our adventure with them all along the way.

What follows is a catalogue of the artworks with descriptions by Rob, interspersed with photographs by Amanda and a map. The remaining original artworks and prints are available to view at the Natural Gallery if you are in the vicinity of Solva.

When next in Spain or Portugal consider going inland to these fabulous places. We are sure you would find it well worth a visit.

If you are not able to get to the gallery and would like to find out whether an original painting is still available, price information, or order a print please point your phone camera at the QR code next to each artwork (not too close), and you will be taken to the correct gallery web page.

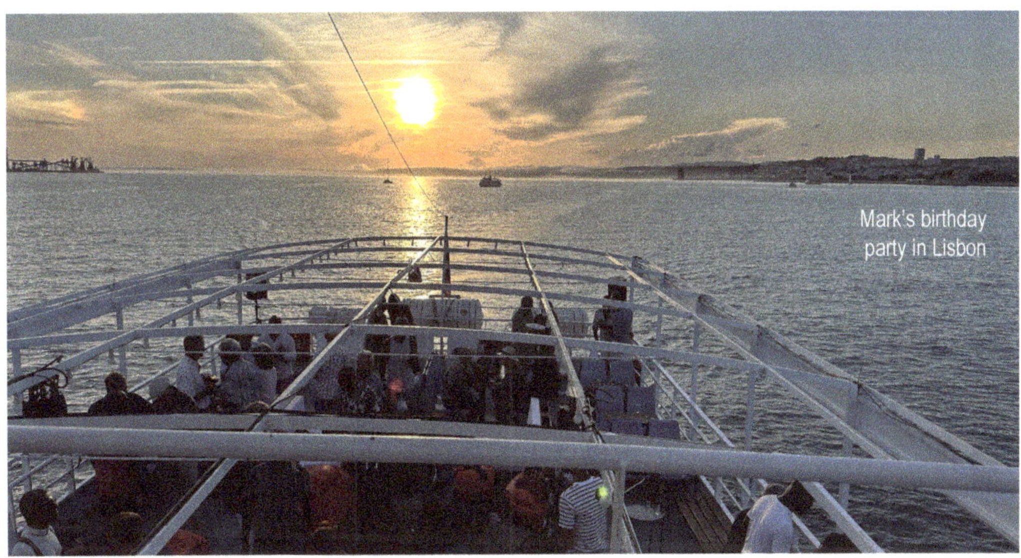

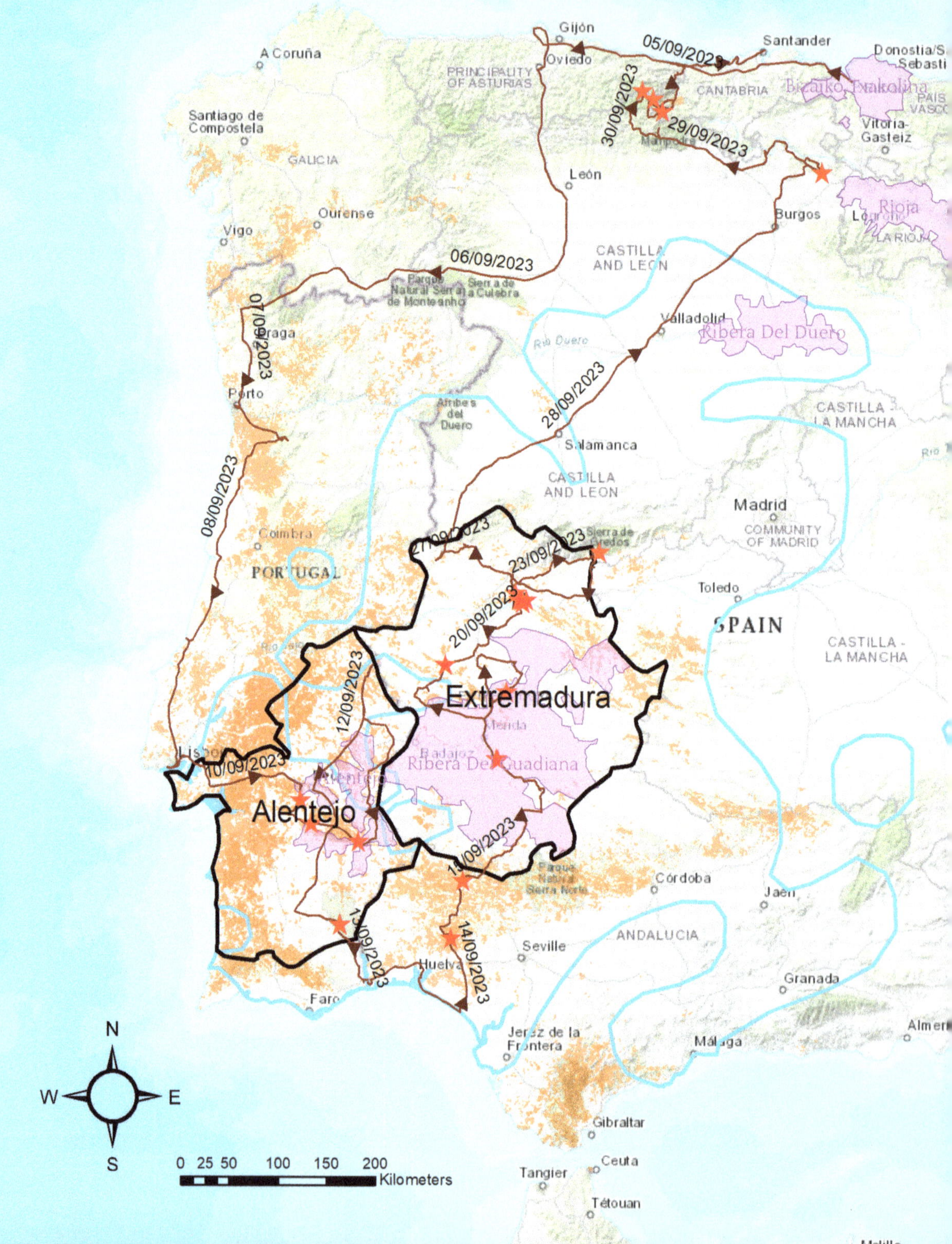

Service Layer Credits: Sources: Esri, HERE, Garmin, Intermap, increment P Corp., GEBCO, USGS, FAO, NPS, NRCAN, GeoBase, IG
Kadaster NL, Ordnance Survey, Esri Japan, METI, Esri China (Hong Kong), (c) OpenStreetMap contributors, and the GIS User Comm
Gijón
Santander
Donostia/S.
Sebasti
Oviedo
05/09/2023
A Coruña
PRINCIPALITY
OF ASTURIAS
CANTABRIA
Bizkaiko Txakolina
PAIS
VASCO
30/09/2023
29/09/2023
Vitoria-
Gasteiz
Santiago de
Compostela
Manzara
GALICIA
León
Rioja
Burgos
LA RIOJA
Ourense
06/09/2023
CASTILLA
AND LEON
Vigo
Valladolid
Ribera Del Duero
Parque
Natural Serra Culebra
de Montesinho
Sierra de
Río Duero
07/09/2023
Braga
28/09/2023
CASTILLA
LA MANCHA
Porto
Arribes
del
Duero
Río
Salamanca
CASTILLA
AND LEON
08/09/2023
Madrid
Coimbra
COMMUNITY
OF MADRID
Sierra de
PORTUGAL
redos
23/09/2023
SPAIN
CASTILLA -
LA MANCHA
20/09/2023
Toledo
12/09/2023
Extremadura
Mérida
Lisboa
10/09/2023
Alentejo
Ribera De Guadiana
Badajoz
Córdoba
Jaén
11/09/2023
Parque
Natural
Sierra Norte
ANDALUCIA
14/09/2023
Seville
Granada
Huelva
Almer
Faro
Jerez de la
Frontera
Málaga
N
W   E
Gibraltar
S
Ceuta
Tangier
0 25 50   100   150   200
Kilometers
Tétouan

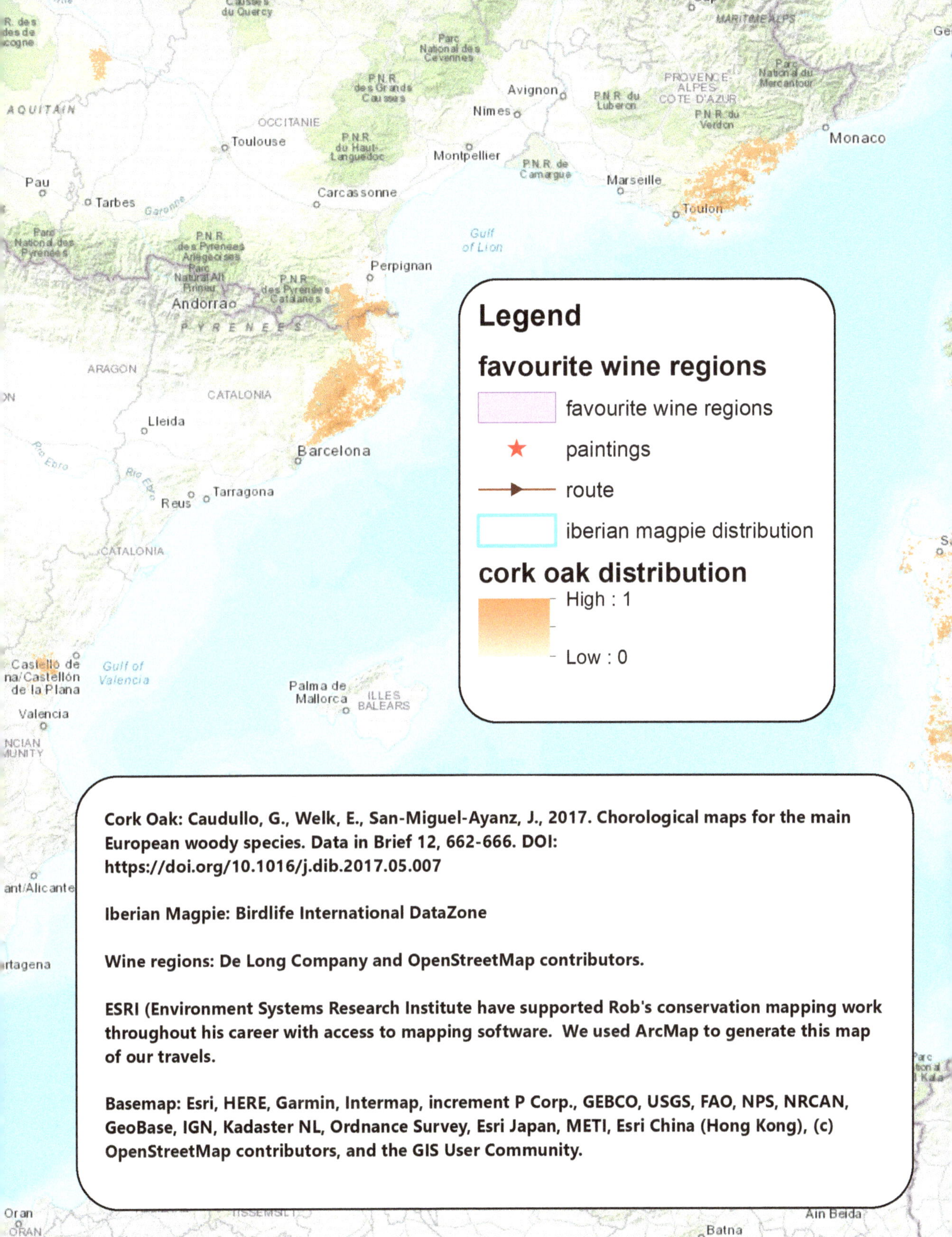

Legend
favourite wine regions
favourite wine regions
paintings
route
iberian magpie distribution
cork oak distribution
High : 1
Low : 0
Cork Oak: Caudullo, G., Welk, E., San-Miguel-Ayanz, J., 2017. Chorological maps for the main European woody species. Data in Brief 12, 662-666. DOI: https://doi.org/10.1016/j.dib.2017.05.007
Iberian Magpie: Birdlife International DataZone
Wine regions: De Long Company and OpenStreetMap contributors.
ESRI (Environment Systems Research Institute have supported Rob's conservation mapping work throughout his career with access to mapping software. We used ArcMap to generate this map of our travels.
Basemap: Esri, HERE, Garmin, Intermap, increment P Corp., GEBCO, USGS, FAO, NPS, NRCAN, GeoBase, IGN, Kadaster NL, Ordnance Survey, Esri Japan, METI, Esri China (Hong Kong), (c) OpenStreetMap contributors, and the GIS User Community.

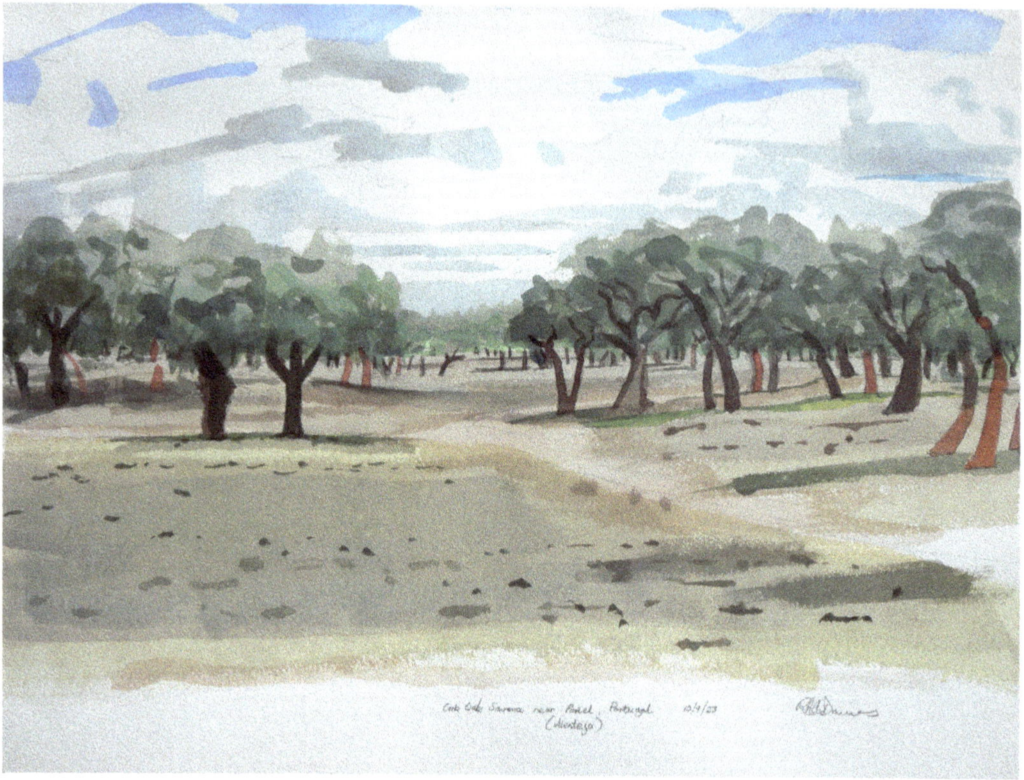

Cork Oak Savanna near Portel

Watercolour on Arches Aquarelle Not 300gsm paper
unframed
77 x 57 cm

This was a lovely open patch of Cork Oak savanna on our first venture into Alentejo, the 'wild outback' of Portugal. I felt such a relief as the landscape changed, becoming more arid and filled with fantastic trees the further East we drove from Lisbon. The Cork Oaks seem to grow in obvious patches, especially where the ground seems raised and more rocky, a broken terrain. Heaven for birds of prey and other wildlife and we met our first Iberian magpies not far from this site. While I sketched, Amanda enjoyed the Hoepoes and larks foraging and singing nearby. Natural habitats such as these sound different from the more man-made landscapes further north. They are alive. Not just birds but botanically rich too. It may look like bare ground under the trees but as many as 135 species of vascular plants have been recorded in one small patch (about 30 x 30m) in a study area of Cork Oak woodland in Andalucia which is one of the highest known plant diversities in the world at this small scale. So it is fortunate that much of these woodlands are protected in Spain and in Portugal either by EU, the State or the landowners who rely on their produce. Even when their bark is harvested as cork, these trees are beautiful with their bare tree trunks glowing the colour of sangria and darkening over time to a burgundy colour.

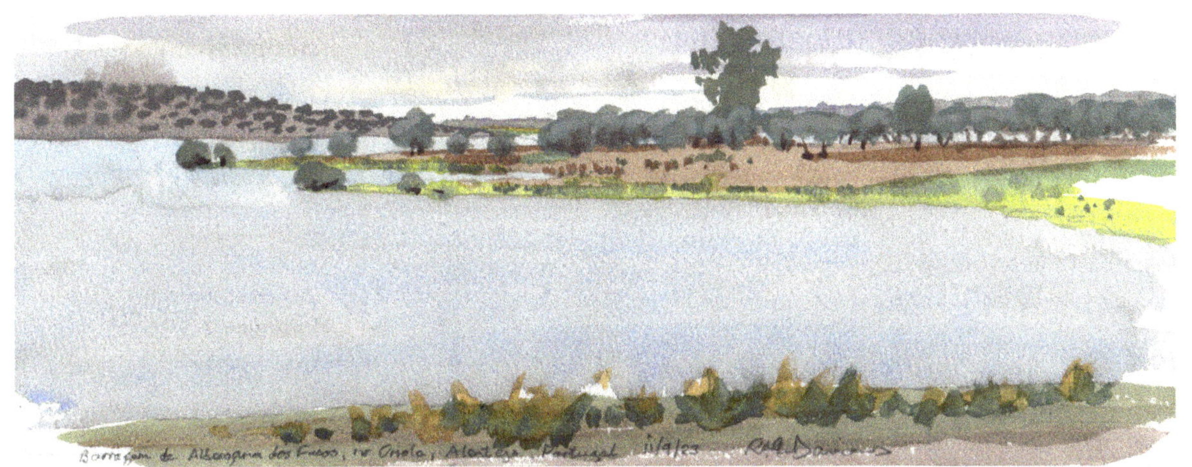

Barragem de Albergaria dos Fusos

Watercolour on Bockingford 300gm2 w/c paper
unframed
42 x 14.8 cm

Our drive into the heartlands of Alentejo on the 10th September was an eye-opener, no more the green-shrouded raptor-less landscapes of northern Portugal - here the colours of the barren earth shone through and natural character returned to the land in the form of the graceful Cork Oak trees leaning at their individual angles. We started seeing and hearing birds again and met our first beautiful Iberian Magpies (previously Azure-winged) - more like blue shrikes as they darted silently from tree to tree. We camped that Sunday night next to this beautiful lake or Barragem near Oriola. Had a great meal in the tiny town that reminded me so much of the places and the people of the Karoo, just a football club in place of a rugby club but the characters looked the same all making their living off this hard land, mostly sheep farmers but here also 'tree farmers'. The view from our camp included the Cork Oak-studded ridges (these tree seem to love growing at angles out of the rockiest outcrops) and the softer lighter grey hues of the Olive Trees cultivated on the sands next to the lake. Here we listened to Little Owls in the night and watched harriers and hoopoes and larks during the day. It was a great introduction.

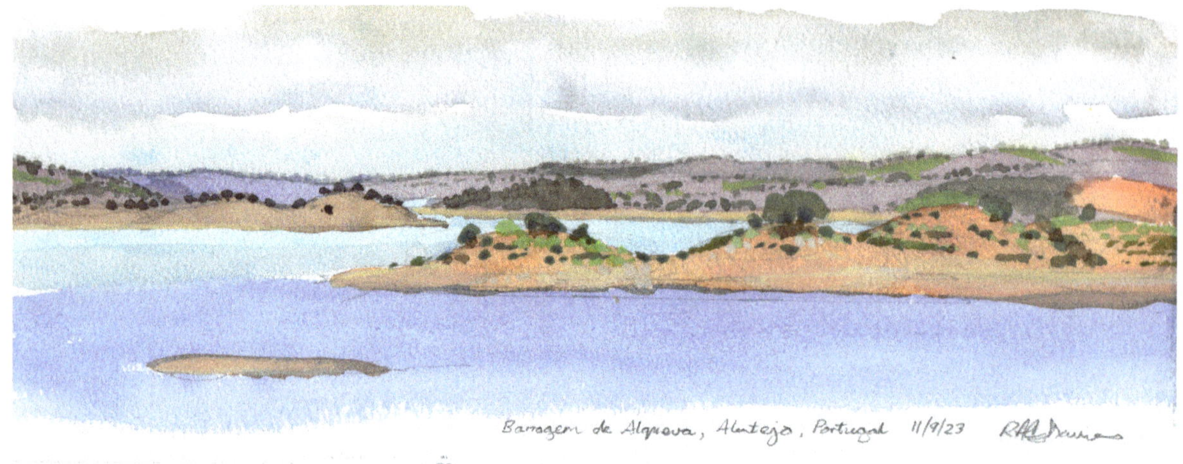

Barragem de Alqueva

Watercolour on Bockingford 300gm2 w/c paper
unframed
43 x 14.8 cm

On the 11th we drove around the South of this very large dam or *Barragem* and as we crossed over the impressive dam wall we stopped to do this watercolour sketch of the wonderful colours of this otherwise dry landscape, and Amanda checked for birds spotting some interesting Waxbills which have colonised Portugal from Africa maybe happy with the warmer climate here now. Cormorants fished nearby. The brighter greens up on the ridges are deceptive, it looks lush but turns out to be patches of a conifer, the Italian Stone Pine. All the trees in this water-limited place are held in a stunted growth form but all fantastic shapes.

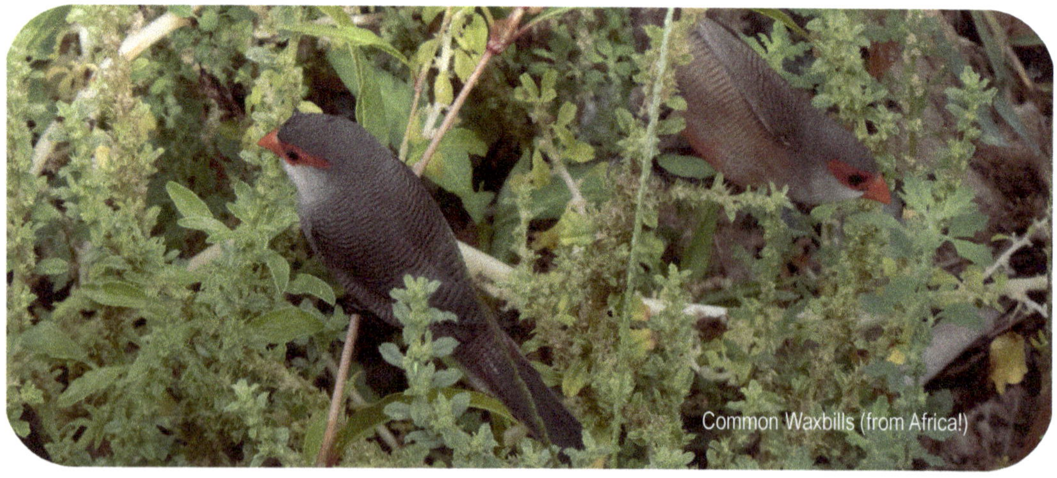

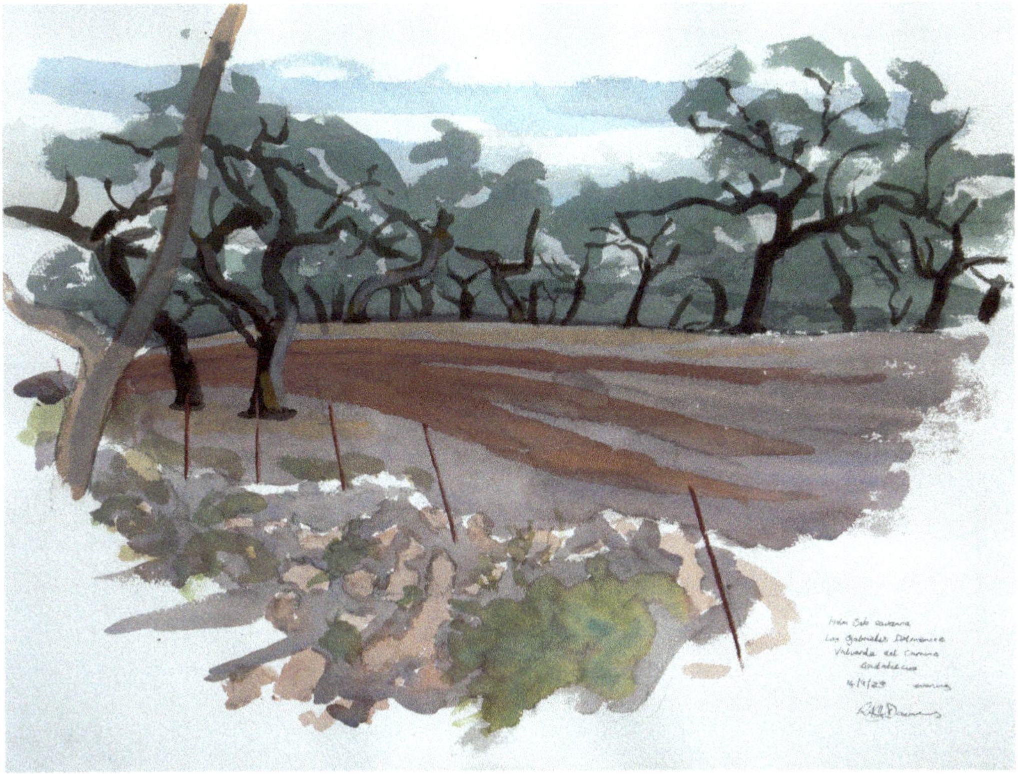

Holm Oak Savanna

Watercolour on Arches Aquarelle Not 300gsm paper
unframed
77 x 57 cm

We found the best way to break into the protected oak savannas was at the ancient dolmen sites. This site, Los Gabrieles Domenico is near Valverde del Camino still in Andulucia just south of Extremadura. It is a wild expanse of Holm Oak savanna. The bare earth appears tilled in some way under the trees presumably to make harvesting the acorns easier and in some areas the land is also cultivated under the trees. Here it was quite wild and natural and when we got to the dolmens we looked out over an enormous valley which must have been the range of the hunter-gatherers who lived here many thousands of years ago. You could see the attraction of the place because they could see everything going on in the entire valley.

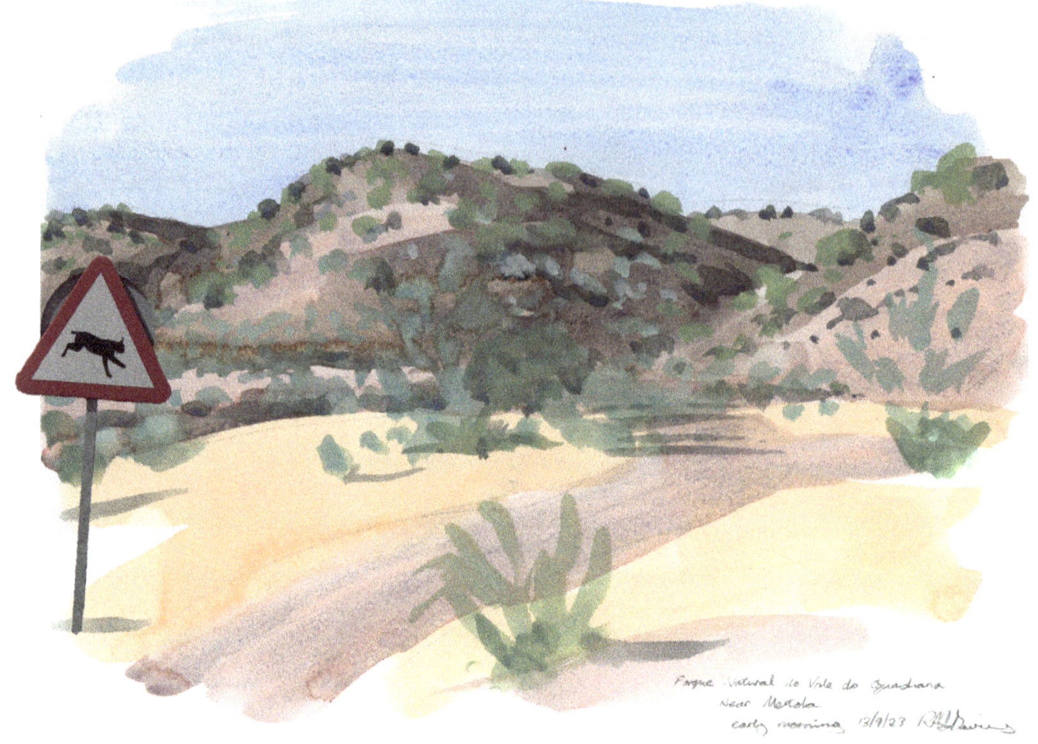

Parque Natural do Vale do Guadiana

Watercolour on Arches 300gm2 100% cotton hot-pressed
watercolour paper
unframed
41 x 31 cm

We were in Iberian Lynx country now. It was exciting to see the traffic calming signs as we came
into the Parque Natural do Vale do Guadiana but we knew there was small chance of seeing
them. I think I had nine sightings of the similar-sized Caracal Lynx in the Karoo National Park
while living there and walking in the mountains daily over a five year period. But we could
hope and we went into 'Lynx' mode searching for sighting or sign. We saw and heard their prey,
a beautiful Fallow Deer hind spied us trustingly from the scrub and we heard partridges moving
up and down the slopes to drink in the river. There is a town in the middle of the park called
Mértola which was a nice lunch stop but we were suddenly inescapably hot - just not used to
the 34 degree temperature. So we found a spot as close to the river as possible to free camp. It
was wonderful there with a friendly Red Fox who came to catch moths around the camp in our
torch lights. In the morning of 13 September I did this small sketch of the broken hillsides as it
got hot and dry very quickly. Amanda went for a walk and photographed some very clear Lynx
signs - bleached white rounded scats. There was a spattering of yellow grass here but we felt
that the whole river basin was a rain shadow. The stunted oaks (grey) and Italian Stone Pines
(pale green) on the hillsides very arid adapted, and around the grass the soft-looking grey shrubs
14   *Retama spharocarpa* which are decidedly spiky and not soft when you inspect them closely.

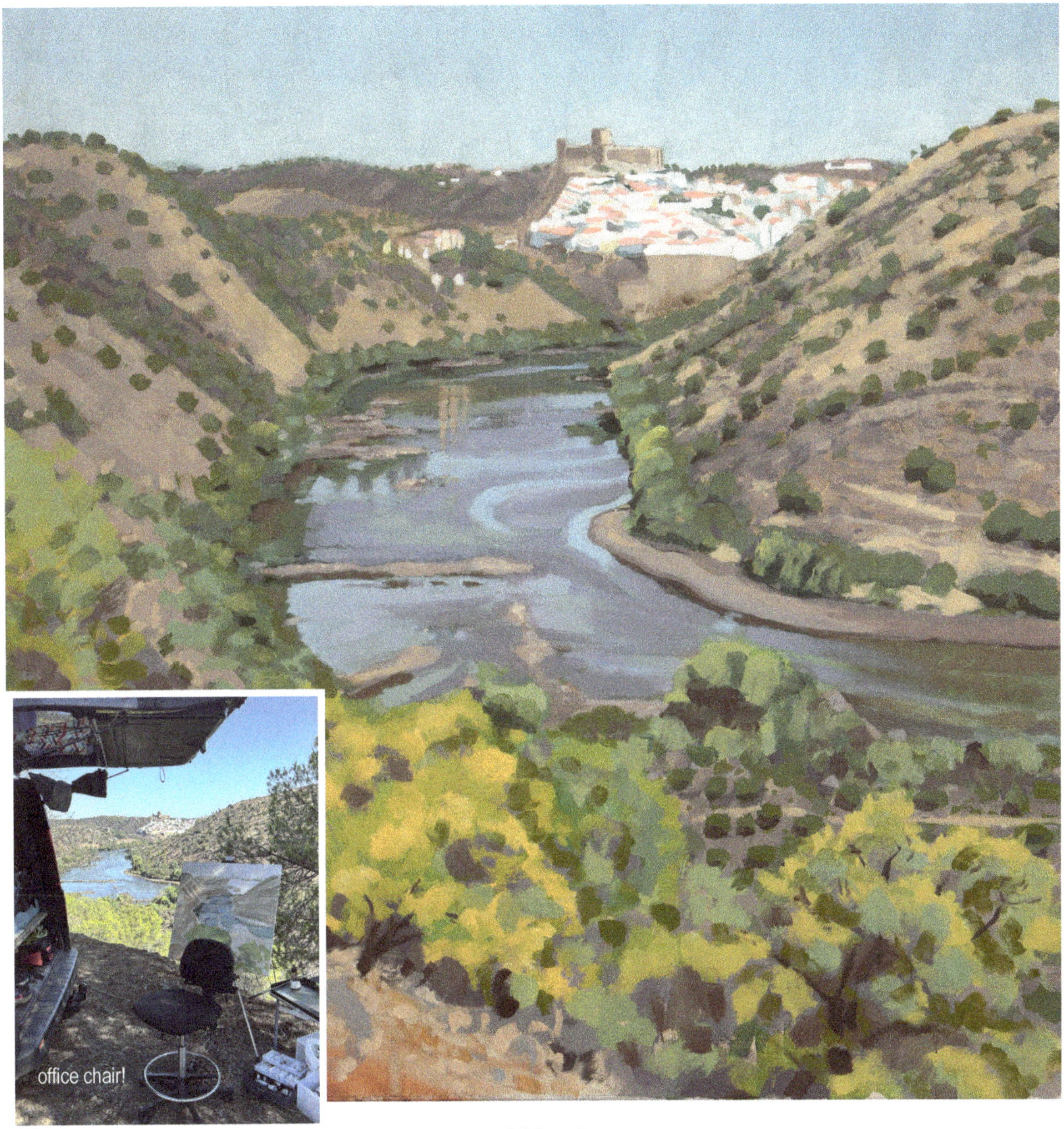

Mértola

Oil on Canvas
unframed
80 x 80 x 2.5 cm

Next, I painted the view back from our campsite to the amazing town of Mértola over the Rio do Guadiana as the sun came over the hill onto the river, but it really did get too hot and I had to pack up after 11 am, so I finished most of this large oil in the studio back home.

Short-toed Eagle

Watercolour and Ink on Arches 300gm2 100% cotton
hot-pressed watercolour paper
unframed
30 x 45 cm

We saw the eagle in this painting just North of Aracena (southern Extremadura) perched on a boulder silhouetted in the early morning sun. Sketched from a distance with the big berthas. It was great to get to grips with a wildlife subject at last. After a while the eagle flew off and was joined by another circling and calling in the valley.

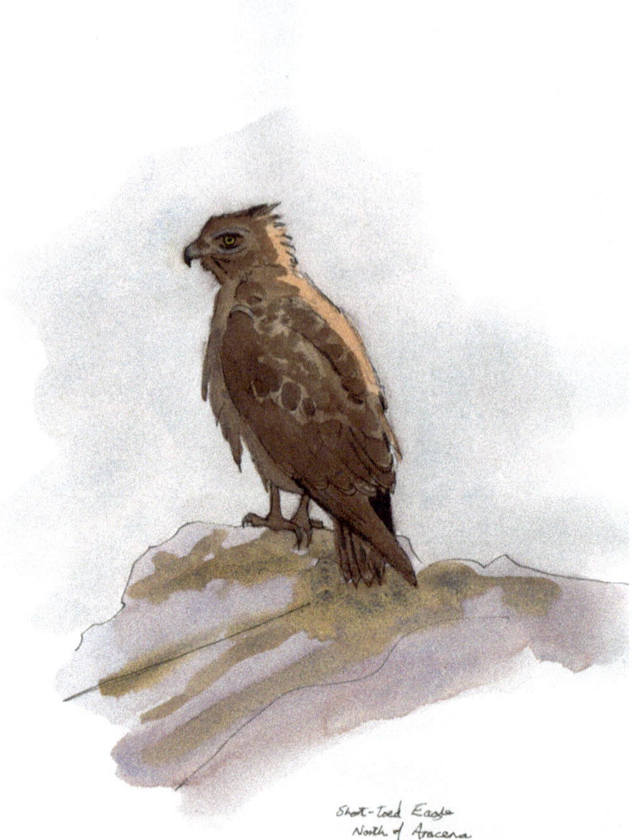

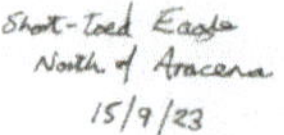

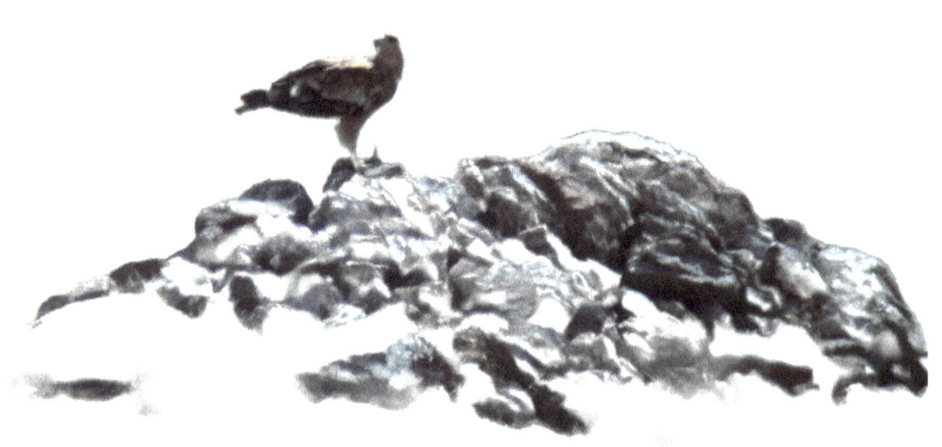

our first Spanish Imperial Eagle, a juvenile with prey

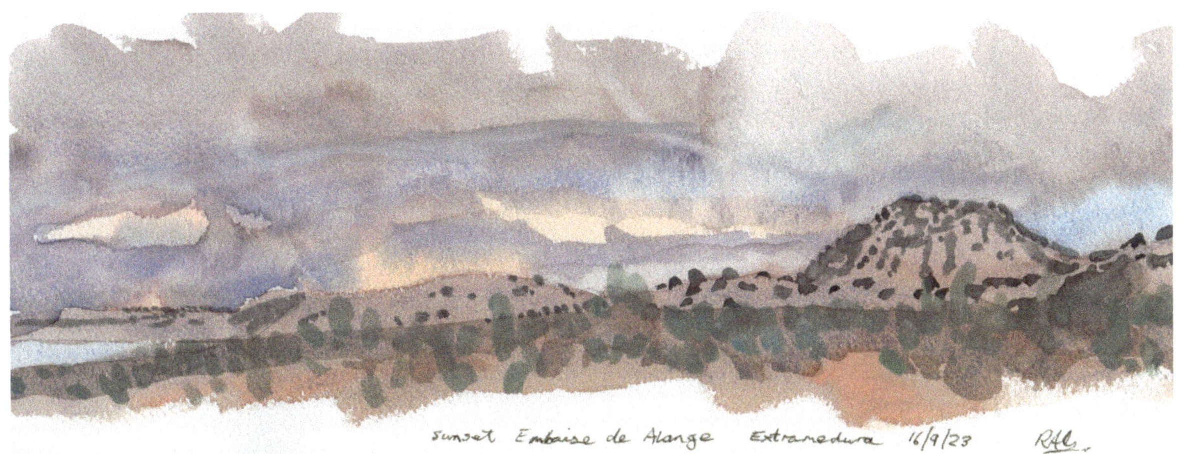

Embaise de Alange sunset

Watercolour on Bockingford 300gsm w/c paper
unframed
43 x 14.8 cm

Although we couldn't reach the strongholds of the Iberian Lynx to the South and East of Spain in Cordoba and Sierra Morena this trip we did do a major detour East into the Matachel Valley which makes a great habitat corridor for these animals connecting to their strongholds in the West. As we headed out onto the barren grassy plain of eastern Extremadura Amanda exclaimed 'what's that!?' as a large shape plummeted out of the sky not far from us, this large pale ochre bird fell from the sky with talons out and secured something near the ground alighting in the bright heat haze. The first time we had ever met the Spanish Imperial Eagle, a young one. We watched it pluck its catch, consume it and spiral back up into the heavens on forceful thermals and it disappeared back into its high altitude atmosphere within 30 minutes of its debut. After that we spent a long time trying to find a good camp site on the hot plain but there was a lot of security blocking access to anywhere nice so we headed North again towards Caceres and found this idyllic spot next to a lake, Embaise de Alange. Surrounded by Griffon mountains in absolute peace and quiet we camped under a Holm Oak tree to a wonderful sunset. It was so nice we stayed a couple of days relaxing in the company of Hoepoes, larks and Marsh Harriers hunting around the lake.

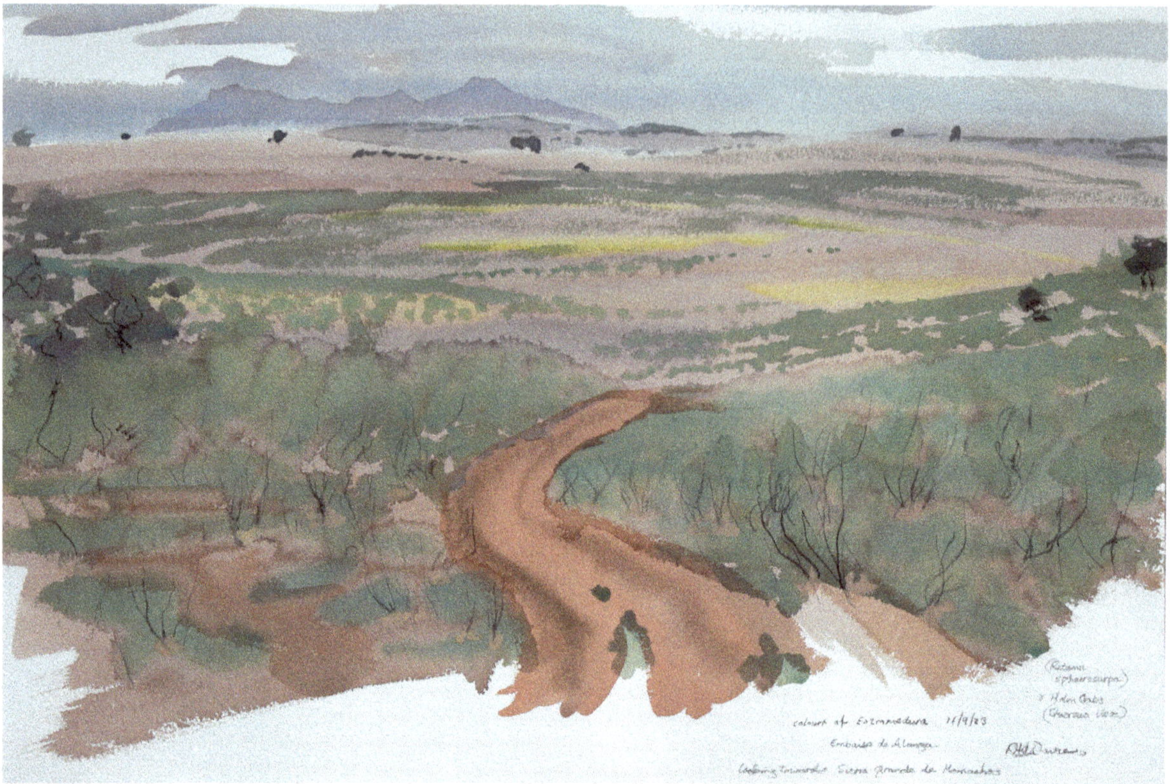

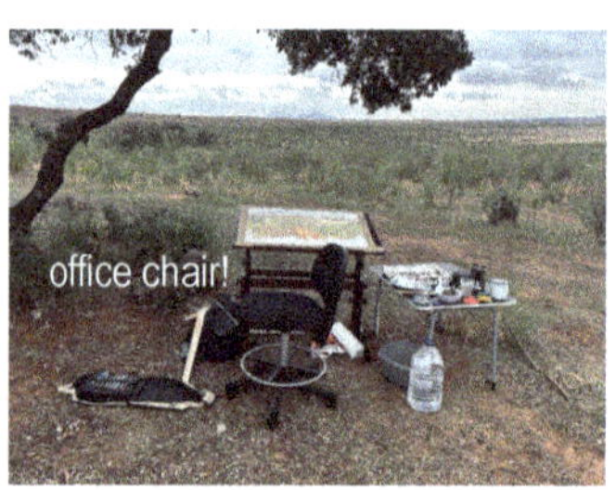

Embaise de Alange colours

Watercolour on Arches Aquarelle Not 300gsm paper
unframed
77 x 57 cm

Sitting out under the Holm Oak we camped under, with the art board and my rather out-of-place office chair, it was an ideal spot to stretch a large piece of Arches watercolour paper and try to capture the textures and soft colours of this part of Extremadura. I started off with the paper quite wet and let the colours drift into one another rather like the vegetation does here. The rough texture of the Not pressed paper helped with the distant scrubbiness. It was just so nice to find the purples of the Sierra Grande de Hornachos in the distance, reds of the bare earth and the soft grey greens of the spikey Retama sphaerocarpas that surrounded me. Arid lands just seem to suit my palette so much more than higher rainfall areas! We saw a few vultures, the harriers and listened to the larks around us.

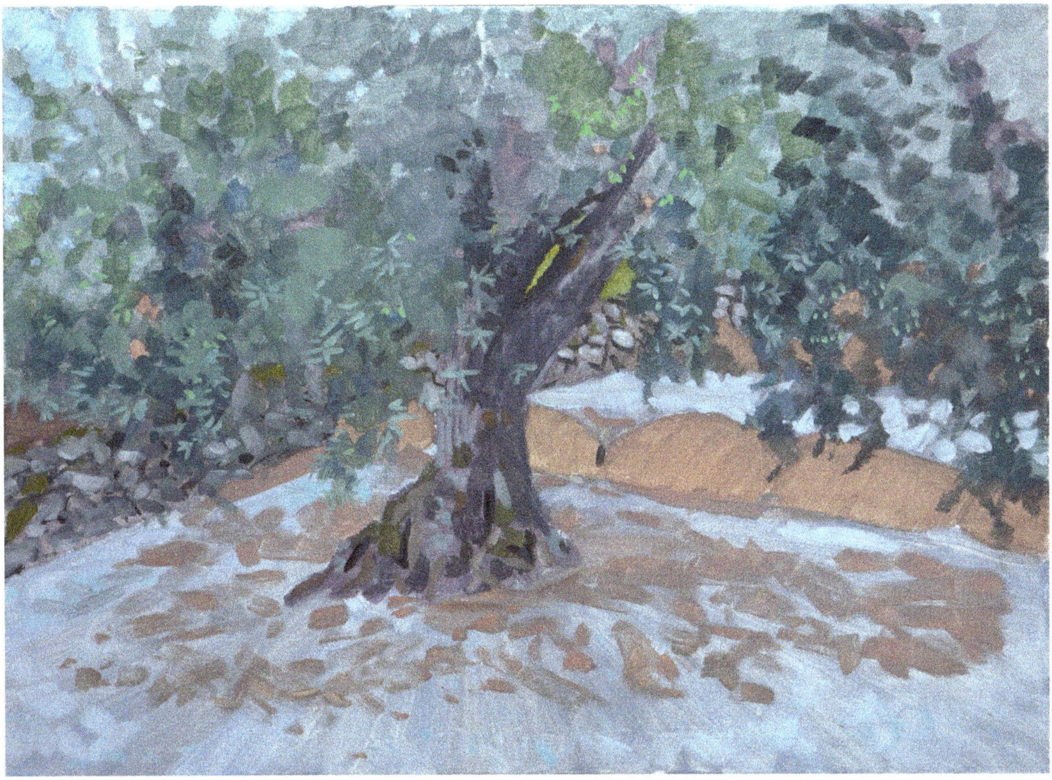

Olive Tree

Oil on Canvas
unframed
70 x 50 x 2 cm

The meaning of the word Dehesa is 'private' and it is the value of these woodlands that preserve the trees and wild inhabitants. Along with the Cork Oaks and the Holm Oaks, Olive trees can also be a very widerspread albeit more cultivated component of these woodland habitats known as Dehesa. Usually the Olives are found planted in rows closer to human habitation but the birds love them too and the Olive trees are just as characterful as the oaks with similar small tough xerophytic leaves, ancient craggy grey barks, but a lighter grey green in their colours.

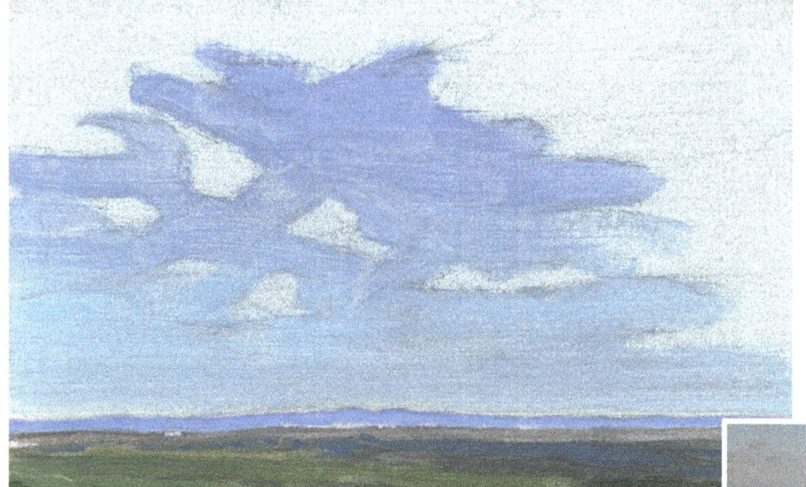

From Sierra de San Pedro, near Aliseda

Oil on Lavender Hill handmade 4mm birch
with linen, unframed
30.5 x 40.8 x 0.5 cm

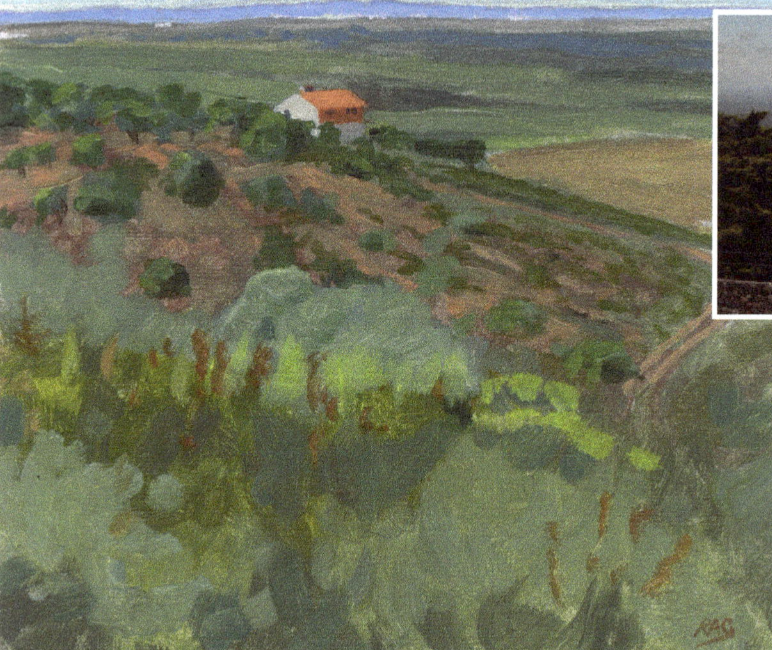

To Sierra de San Pedro
from Marvao in Portugal

When our friend Paddy Waller joined us for hiking we set off first to see the Sierra de San Pedro mountain range which is rich in biodiversity and comprises part of a big trans-frontier conservation area (we had seen these mountains from the amazing *Marvao* lookout in the Portuguese component). It's supposed to be great for raptors in fact we first explored around the Embalse de la Peña del Águila a large lake carrying their name. We saw Short-toed Eagles, many Griffon Vultures and, through the big berthas, a stunning pair of Egyptian Vultures perched atop a very distant rock outcrop. But it was this villa / farmstead that caught my eye standing out in bright Sienna against the beautiful blue expanses of northern Extremadura plains beyond. You can just make out the white and pink urban shine of Plasencia against the distant blue Gredos marking the northern boundary of this amazing province. The plains are transected by the Rio Salor but I really liked the soft green foreground vegetation colours against the bare earth substrate colours.

Bonelli's Eagles
Monfrague National Park

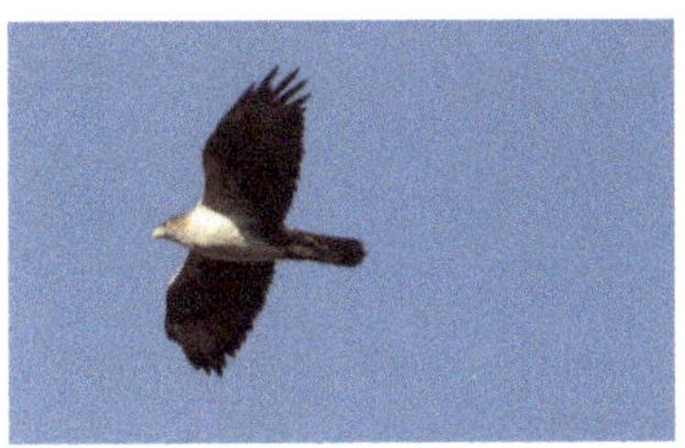

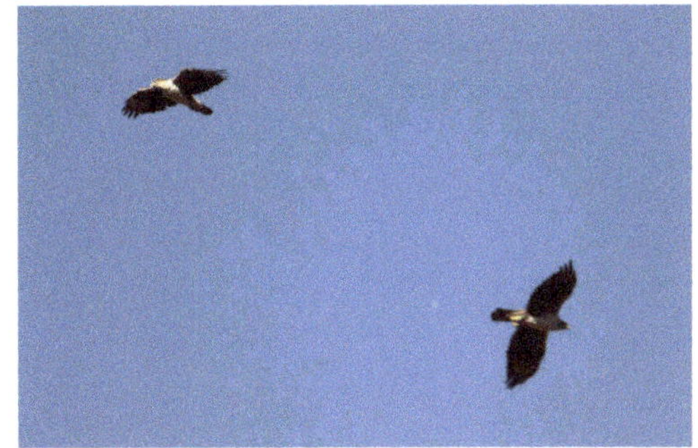

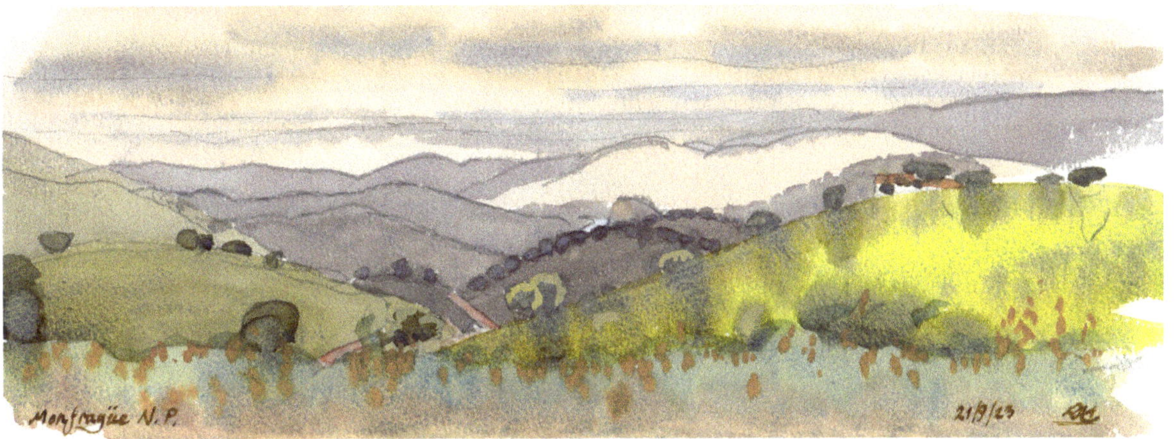

Monfrague National Park, Villarreal de San Carlos, looking East

Watercolour on Bockingford 300gm2 w/c paper
unframed
42 x 14.8 cm

This is the view from the little village, Villarreal de San Carlos in the middle of Monfrague National Park looking East across the park on one rainy afternoon. You can see a sliver of the dam that snakes through the park and the wonderful staccato silhouette of oak trees lining the hill tops.. great habitat for Bonelli's Eagles and Black Vultures which can be seen clearly from the roads. This little national park in Spain is the closest equivalent in Europe to a game reserve experience in Africa. Lots of Red Deer everywhere. Hunting has been permitted in parts of the park which is why they know Iberian Lynx occur here because one was treed by dogs recently. There has been a public outcry to stop hunting in the park.

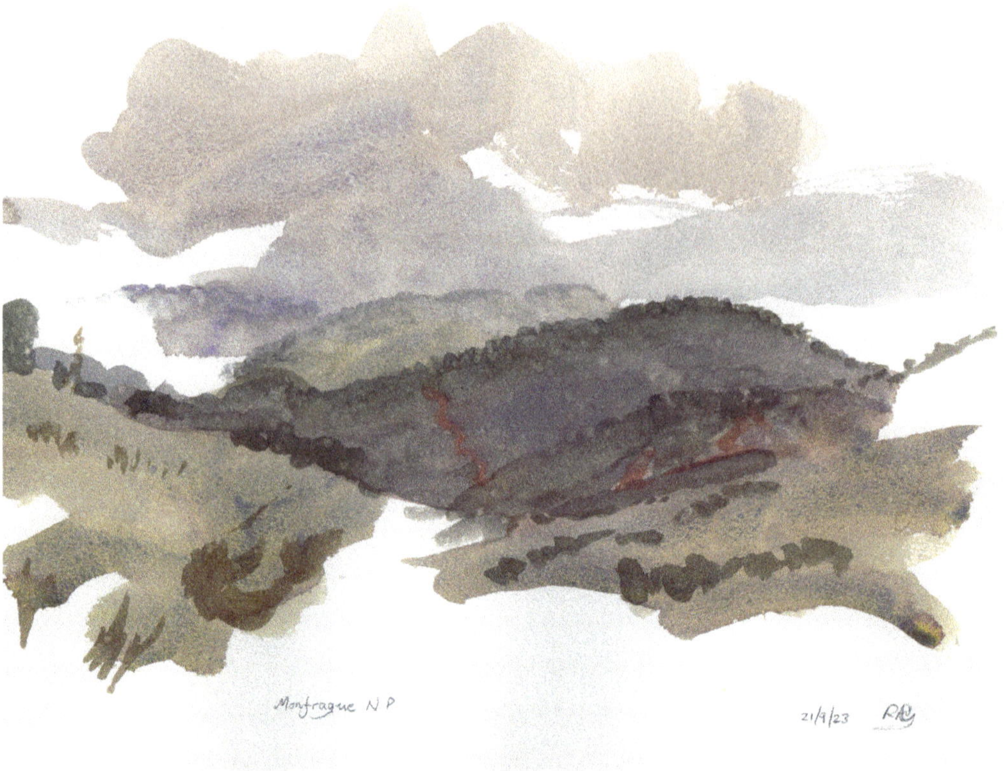

Monfrague National Park, Villarreal de San Carlos, looking West

Watercolour on Bockingford 300gm2 w/c paper
unframed
30.5 x 45 cm

This is the view from the village, Villarreal de San Carlos in the middle of Monfrague National Park looking West on one rainy afternoon.

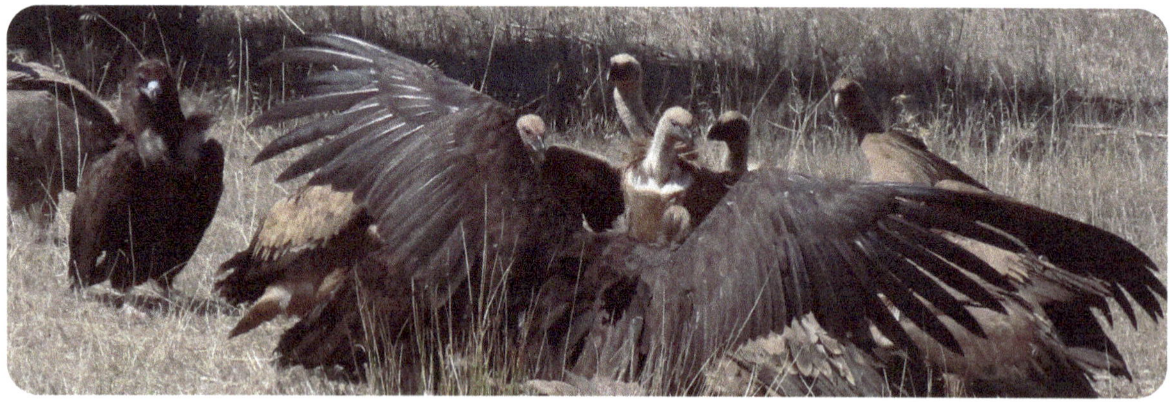

we witnessed this fantastic gathering of Black and Griffon Vultures at a cow carcase near the road in Portugal

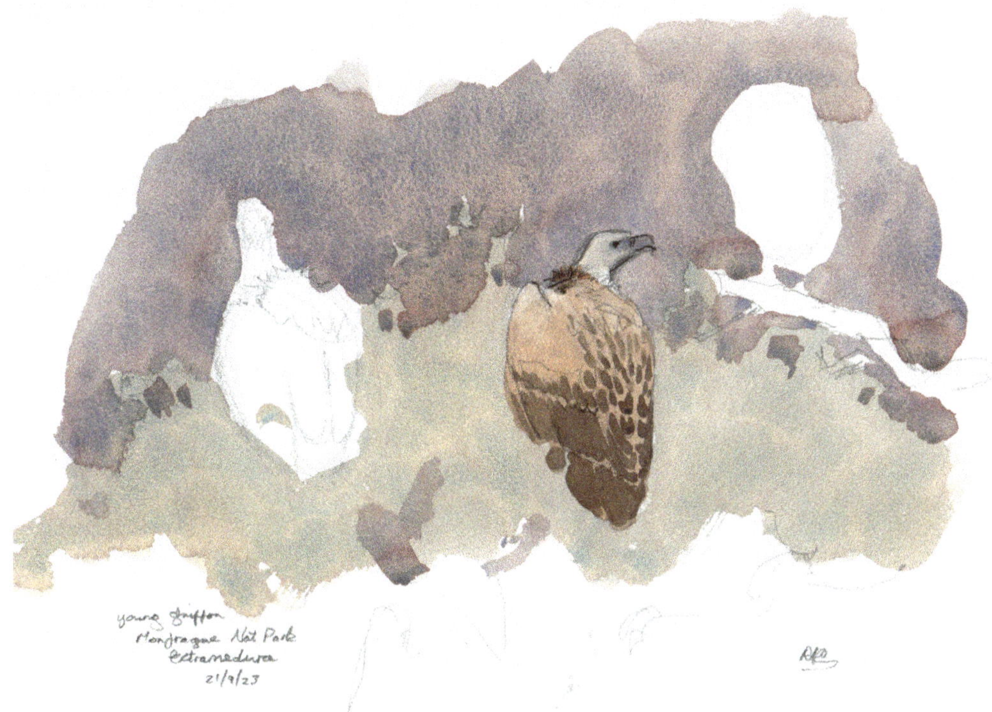

Absent vultures

Watercolour & Gouache on Fabriano cotton cold pressed
300gm2
unframed
51 x 35 cm

We overnighted in a hotel for a change just outside the park so that I could do an early dawn raid of sketching while the wildlife were active. Unfortunately the gate to the hotel was locked so I had to sit there and wait till 9am. There was no sign of the rutting Red Deer stag we had watched last night but I did manage to find this trio of young Griffons enjoying the morning sun on a treetop near the river. It was a great composition and I pencilled in the outlines before settling to study the middle bird. So full of character they are. Then the two flankers did what birds do they flew away! So it wasn't my lucky day and a work in progress but I enjoyed watching these youngsters up to mischief starting their day. I got the impression these young vultures have a lot to learn. They are intelligent birds and they must spend a long period of time learning in these small kindergarten groups while the parents forage out hundreds of kilometres from the colony and bring back the 'spicey' meals in their crops. Apparently vultures have the most acidic stomachs and their own antibiotics in their saliva to deal with pathogens and bacteria in their diet. Lose the vultures as we have witnessed in India and the human health cost from pathogens such as rabies and anthrax unchecked can be astronomic and for India ran into billions of dollars over a decade.

Monfrague National Park, after the rains

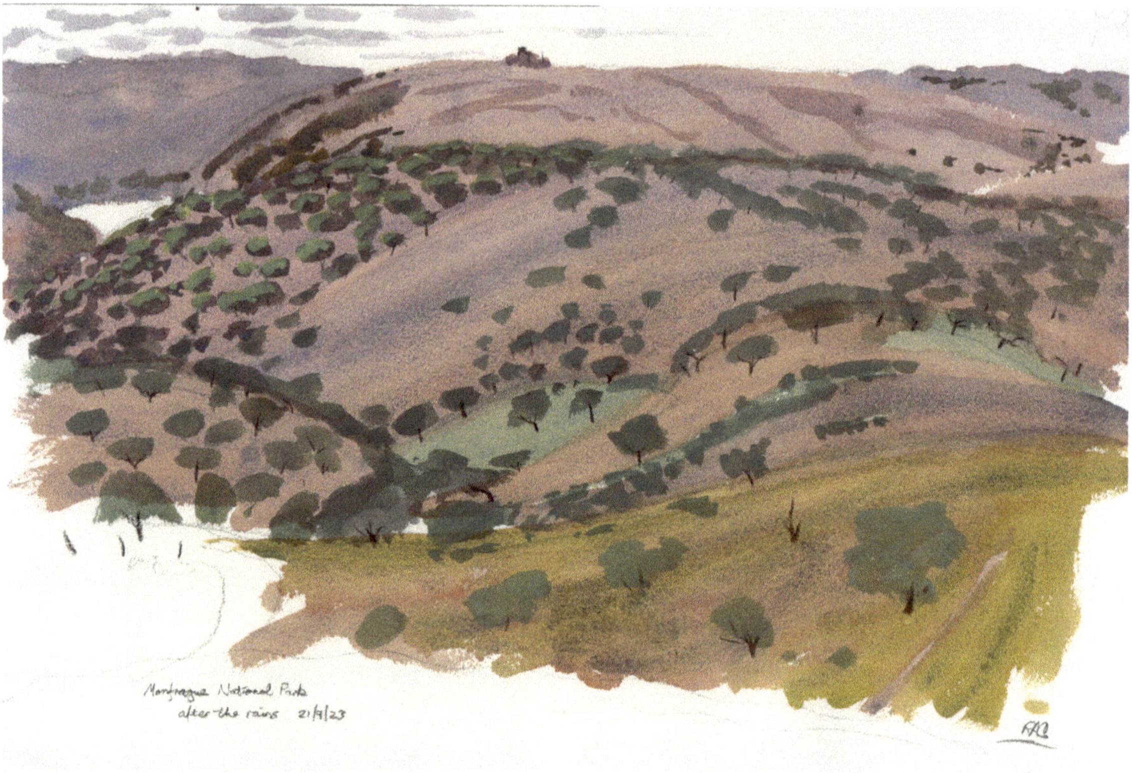

Watercolour on Arches cold-pressed 300gsm
unframed
57 x 38 cm

We were advised to find tame Iberian Magpies in the Parque del Príncipe, Cáceres, by Martin Kelsey and whilst sketching these I was approached by another resident birder who told me Monfrague National Park is very much the destination for birders visiting this region. This is how one birdy thing leads to another! So here we are in the park. It is characterised by an impressive castle on the ridge overlooking the lakes and from there you can look at the vultures eyeball to eyeball. For me though I was still after landscapes and found this view back to the castle past rolling hills and a glimpse of the lake. After rains there was green on the ground as well as the pink bedrocks. With their strong root-holds in the rocks the trees are not impelled to grow upwards as in most forests but can grow out on tough stems at pretty much any angle they prefer and this seems to be a personal choice although I guess they are maximising their light by facing their canopies as much as possible towards the light. As I sketched there were Red Deer rutting and moaning below from the trees. The park is packed with animals, the roads are good, you can stop from them and absorb this natural wonder, so I really felt as much as is possible in Europe, that I was in a game reserve almost like Africa.

Griffon

Watercolour on Arches 300gm2 100% cotton
hot-pressed watercolour paper
unframed
31 x 41 cm

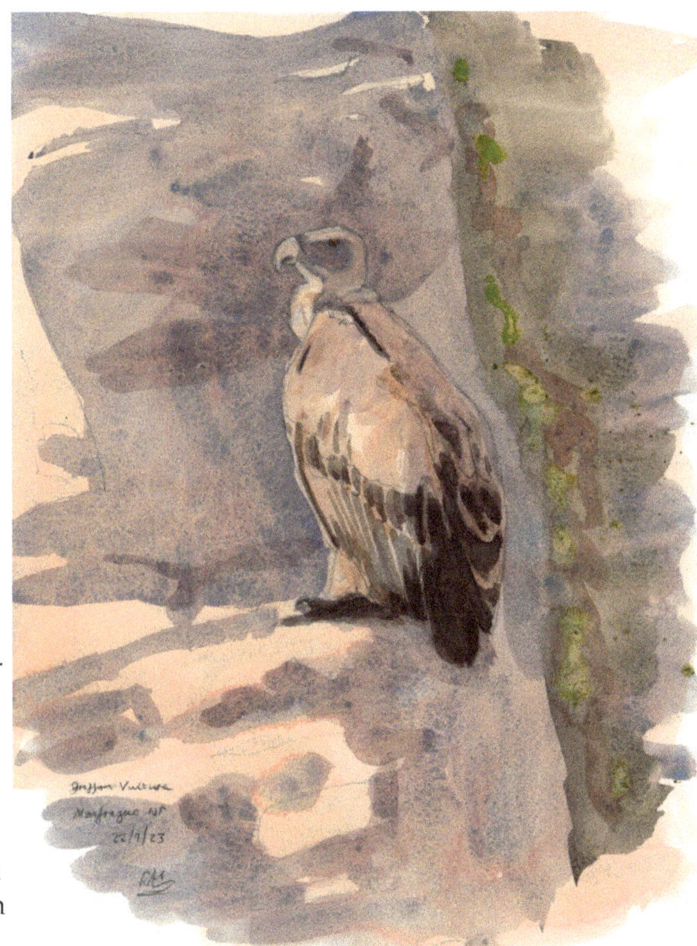

Throughout our journey we were amazed at the sheer volume of the vultures we saw in Spanish skies. Nearly every major hill with cliffs had an adornment of wheeling or perched giant birds. They are only giant when you get the chance to meet them eyeball to eyeball so-to-speak as we did in Monfrague National Park. This is such a success story for Spain to reinstate the keystone ecological role of scavengers which clean the landscape, help prevent the spread of diseases. Griffon Vultures were down to only 5000 pairs in Spain a few decades ago but are now stable / growing at 30,000 pairs. This is despite Spain being ahead of most nations in deploying masses of giant wind turbines along its mountain tops which can sometimes kill raptors in great numbers. In Andalusia there is a specialist team whose job it is to spy approaching vultures and send emergency calls to the wind farms which then shut down turbines. The population seems to overcome these sort of losses and poisonings and thrive. The key must be food and the practice of leaving out carcases for the scavengers. Paddy told me that in places where transhumance and sheep farming are no longer practised there the vultures may decline. But in Extremadura, in the Cork Oak savanna they have a stronghold because it is a healthy functioning ecosystem being maintained that way by the land-owners. The spacing of the oak trees must be perfect for them - enough trees to support wildlife and roosting vultures but not so dense that they cannot run along the ground with a full crop of carrion and get airborne again. In Monfrague National Park, on the rock outcrops, they nest in good numbers and we were able to watch some of their fascinating behaviours at close hand. When I illustrated this species for the field guide I really battled to get the right sandy ochre colour on their backs which can be quite salmon on adult birds, matching their sandstone substrate. This one gave me the chance to find the right hue.

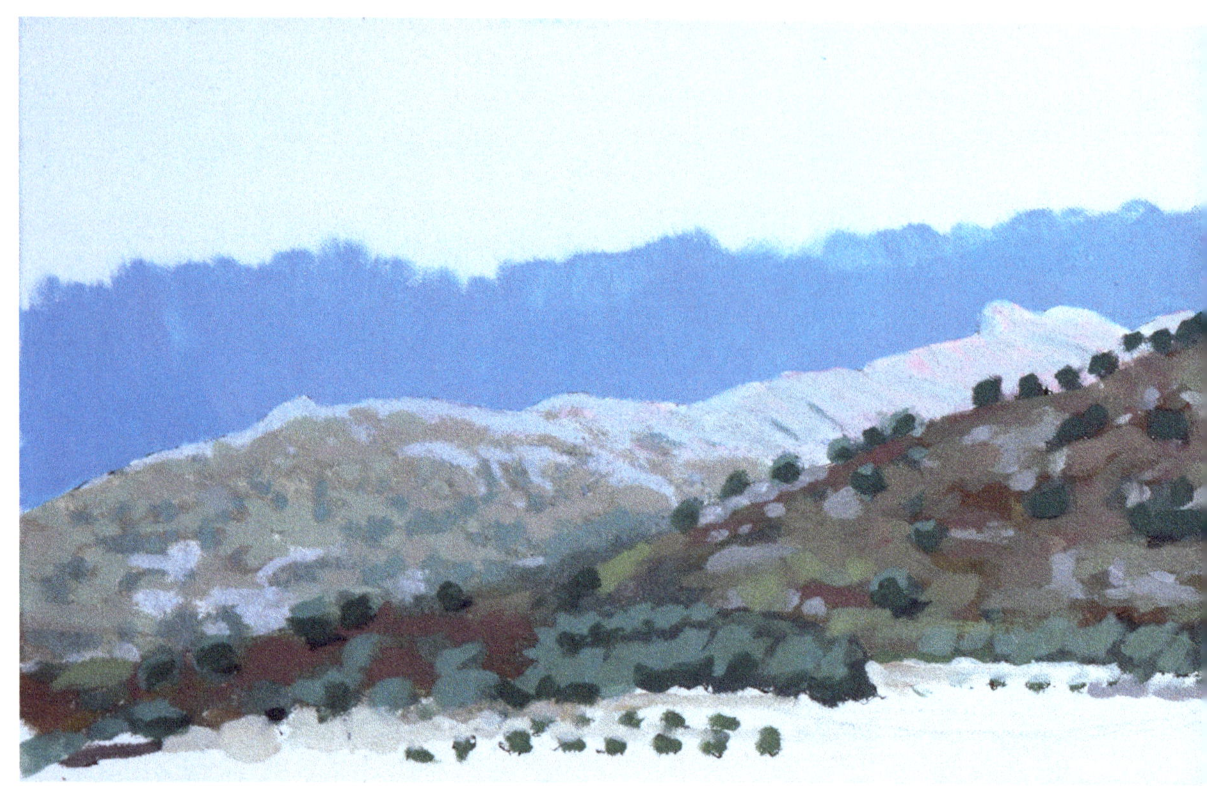

Sierra de Los Gredos

Sierra de los Gredos

Oil on canvas
unframed
100 x 30 cm

There are many mountain ranges or Sierras in Spain but only four can be considered major: Pyrenees, Picos del Europa, Sierra Nevada and the Sierra de Los Gredos which extend westward from Madrid and form the northern barrier boundary to the region of Extremadura. Pico Almanzor rises to 2592m above sea level. Our friend Paddy Waller joined us as we headed to Los Gredos on 23 September 2023 for a 'serious hike' up into these big mountains. It is a fabulous landscape with a sun-bleached pink hue to the top peaks which leap out against the deep blue skies. There is something about the granite rocks that produces incredibly beautiful emerald green waters in the rivers and cascada flowing down the gullies. The hillsides are dotted with oak trees just like further South but with the higher rainfall in the mountains these oaks are much larger and leafier Pyreneen Oaks, *Quercus pyrenaica*, which produces copious acorns like its cousin the Holm Oak. Los Gredos is a regional reserve where Iberian Lynx and wolves find refuge in the wild peaks. We watched Griffon Vultures, Booted Eagle and a Kestrel overhead.

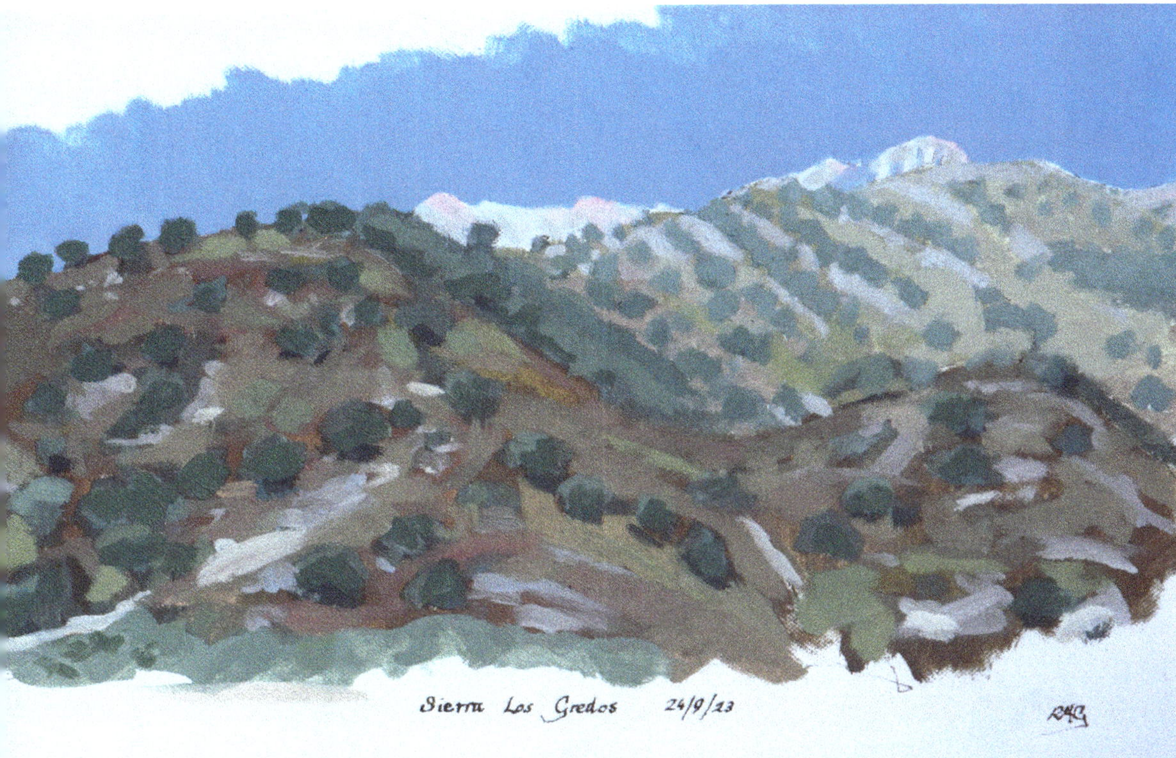

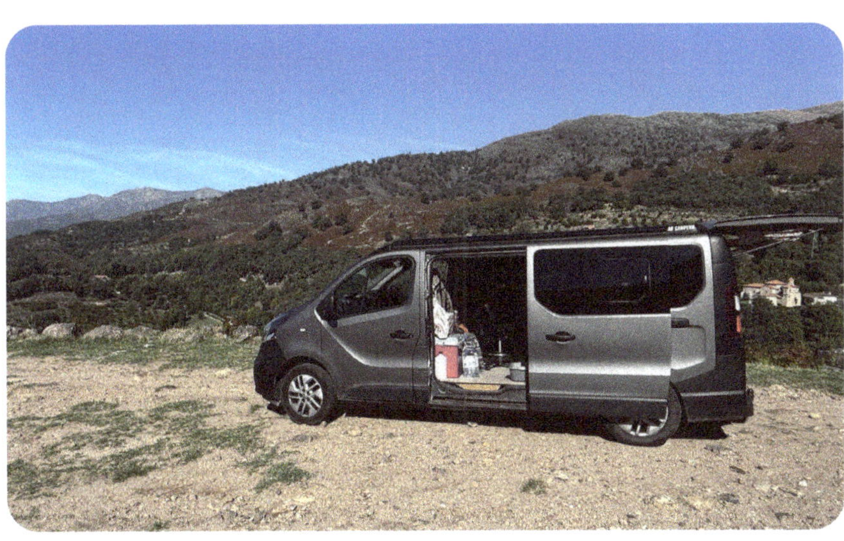

Sierra Los Gredos   24/9/13

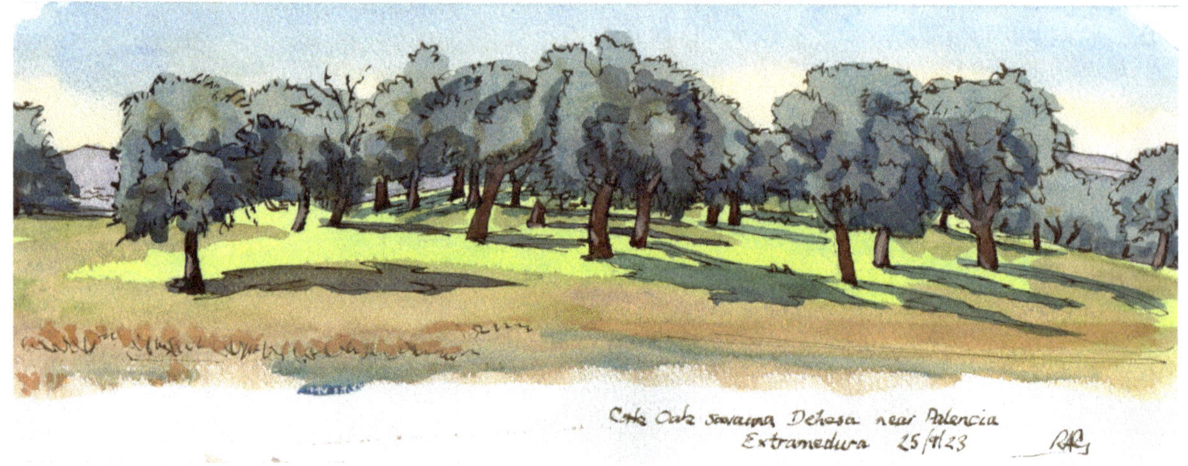

Cork Oaks near Plasencia

Watercolour and Ink on Bockingford 300gm2 w/c paper
unframed
42 x 14.8 cm

I love the way cork oak trees lean out at different angles, especially on top of a slight mound like this. After the rains there are patches of bright green vegetation growing beneath the trees, so reminiscent of camelthorns in the Kalahari. Always a richness of birds and bird song around these trees. I think we saw an adult Spanish Imperial Eagle soar off to great height in the distance. Sketched these to a backdrop of Wood Larks and Thekla's Larks calling and displaying.

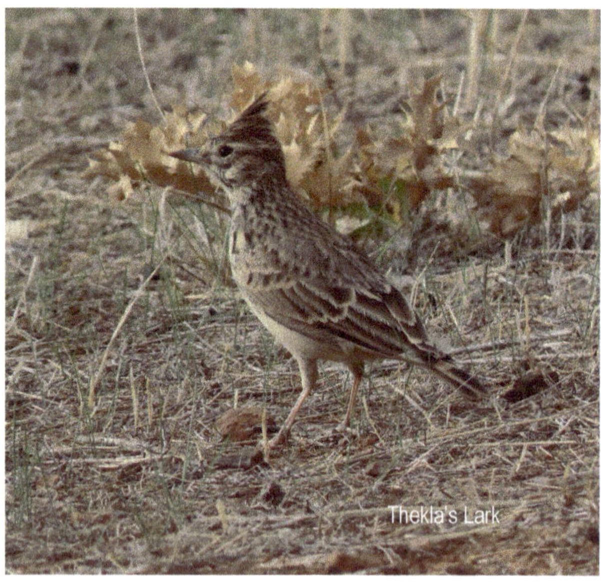

Griffon sketch

Watercolour and Ink on Fabriano cotton cold pressed
300gm2
unframed
51 x 35.5 cm

Adult Griffon Vulture perched on the small cliff (Krantz) near the dam at Monfrague National Park 25/9/2023. We had to wait in Plasencia for a couple of days to source and fit a new windscreen for Myfanwy, so it was a great opportunity to get to know the vultures a bit better. Tried this one in an acrylic raw umber ink with some wash..

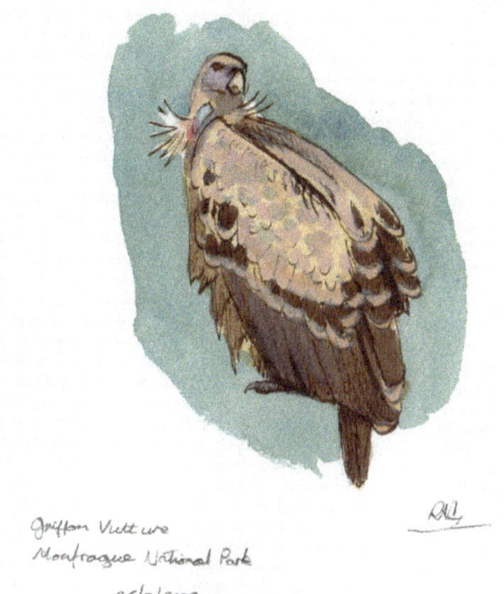

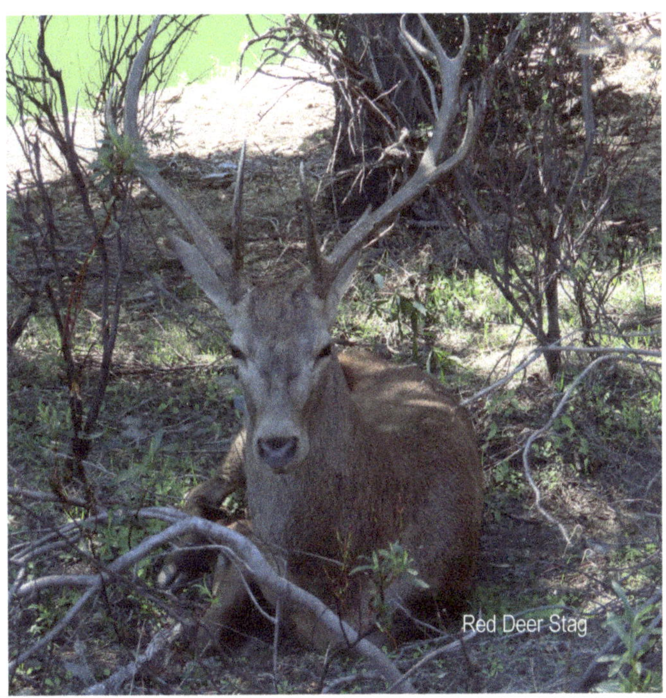

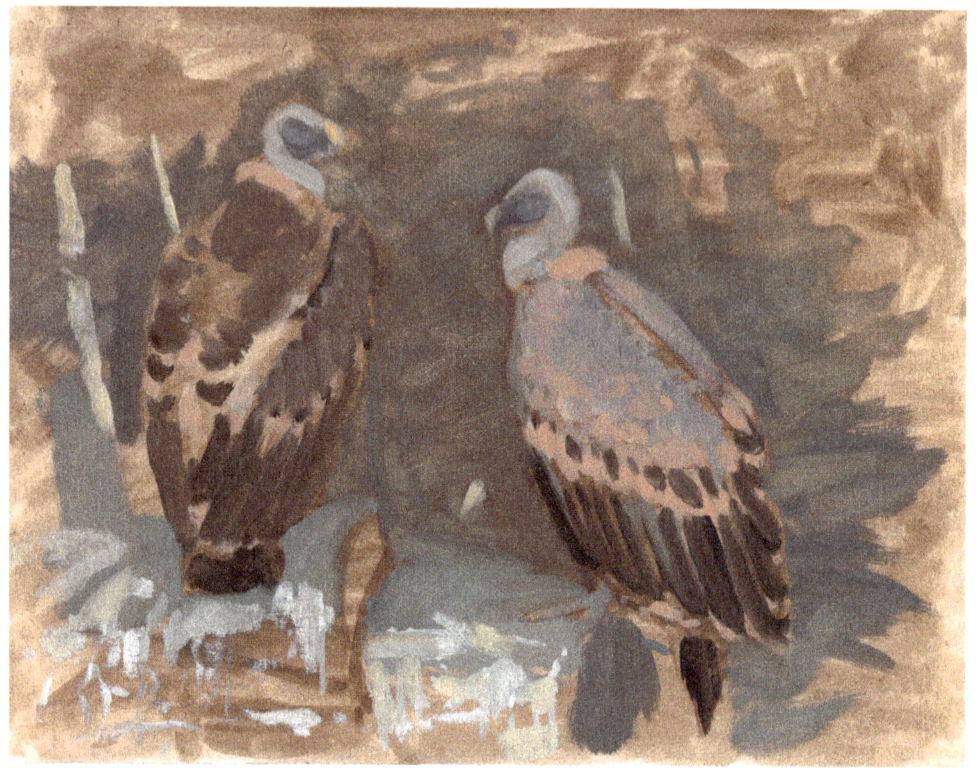

Griffon pair

Oil on Canvas Board
unframed
40.5 x 30.3 x 0.3 cm

This pair of adult Griffon Vultures had classic plumage especially the one on the right with beautiful red tinge, the lefthand bird was darker brown. They looked great against the rock cliff and appeared to have known each other a long time. Their adult status indicated by the ochre horn of their bills and the neat mantles. The vultures were at various stages of breeding. This pair seemed to be settling to nest while another pair had a full-grown chick in their nest and others had fledged successfully. There was a gang of young birds on the top of the cliff that just seemed to be growing up in a playful vulture way, eyeing everything in the sky that passed and going on short sorties with their mates (pals). Youngsters are also quite reddish but with dark bills, spikey (lanceolate) mantle feathers and pointy feather endings all over.

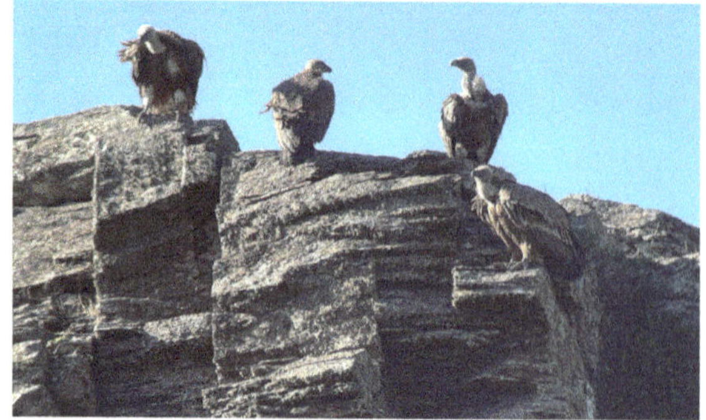

young Griffon Vultures

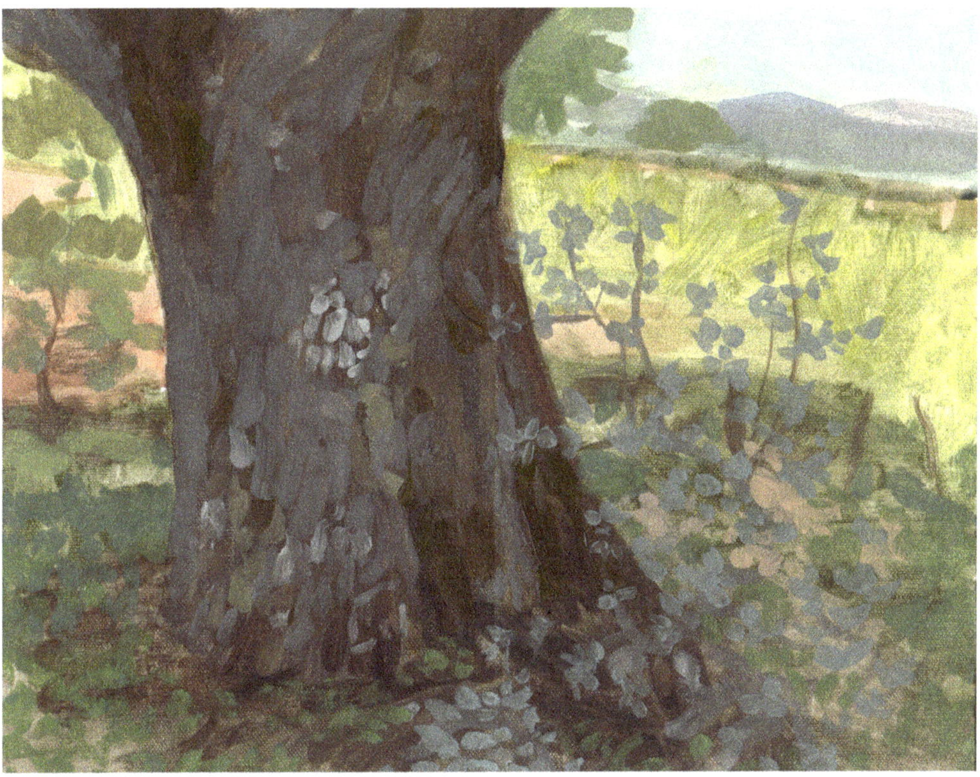

Holm Oak

Oil on Canvas Board
unframed
40.5 x 30.3 x 0.3 cm

At a distance Holm Oak *Quercus ilex* savanna looks just like Cork Oak savanna with the same character-full trees leaning out at all angles, but when you get closer you see the bark is more finely tesselated and you don't get the harvested tree trunks. You do get acorns though in huge profusion and these feed myriad wildlife and livestock on the bare earth below. We did see a couple of Wild Boar a bit earlier (my first) and one dead one on the road. Much more visible were the similar dark Iberian pigs which graze the acorns and give up the famous flavoured jámon that you see hanging from the ceilings in many hostels and homes. While we sat having a picnic lunch under this tree there was a loud 'plop!' - the tree dropped one of its acorns into Amanda's orange juice - a nice memento from Monfrague.

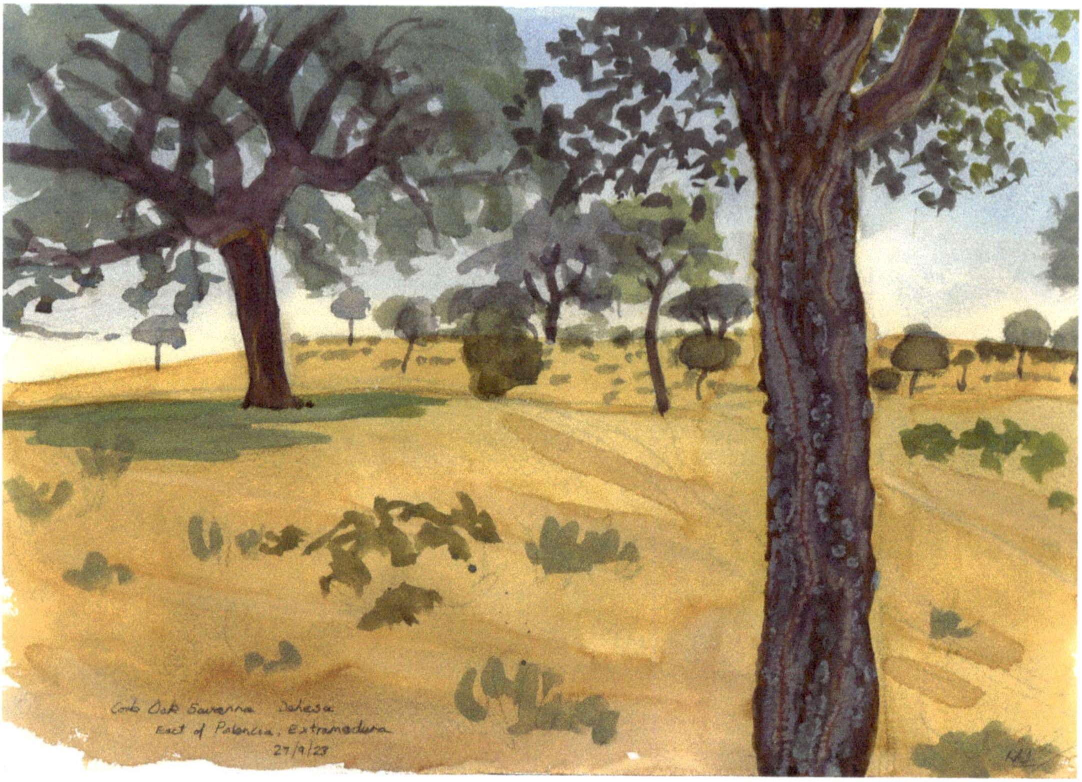

Cork Oak Savanna East of Plasencia

Watercolour & Gouache on Fabriano cotton cold pressed
300gm2
unframed
51 x 35 cm

The bark of the Cork Oak *Quercus suber* is fire-adapted. It protects the sensitive vascular tissues of the tree from extreme heat to such a degree that immediately after a fire, this species of tree can spontaneously sprout from multiple places along its stem and branches making it a highly successful competitor in arid, fire-prone environments. The bark, which can grow to the thickness of a human arm, has value and supports a large industry of silviculture or tree-growing in this part of the Mediterranean. Cork oak savannas are incredibly rich biologically and the value in the cork has a beneficial consequence for conservation in that great forests of these trees are protected and manicured by land-owners across Spain and Portugal. But the same property value had a consequence for Amanda and I on our painting trip because every patch of forest is safeguarded by rolls of barbed wire and security gates. We really battled to find places to stop and study these gentle graceful trees, especially those with a natural coat of bark that had not yet been harvested. The unharvested bark has very soft colours and a thick soft texture of peeling greys encrusted with lichens. The bark can be removed every nine years usually, and has to be done in the rainy season. So we were lucky to find this site on our way north out of Extremedura just East of Plasencia where the site was shared with historic dolmens and open to the public to stop and look at. Clearly the trees had been highly significant too to the human ancestors in this special place. We parked in the dense shade under the big harvested Cork Oak to the left of the painting, which had the deep burgundy coloured trunk, and while I painted the scene (van edited out) Amanda was joined by a herd of goats with jangly bells and a beautiful friendly sheep dog following them about.

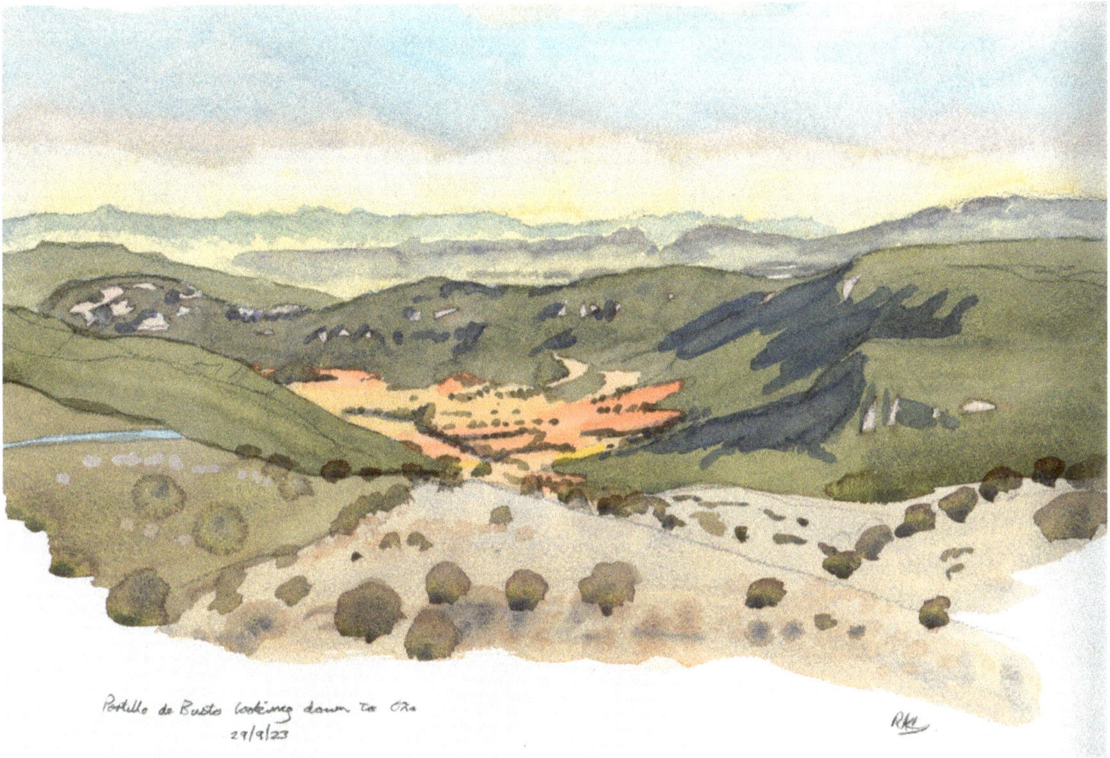

Mirador Portillo de Busto

Watercolour on Fabriano 100% cotton hot-pressed 300gsm
unframed
45.5 x 35.5 cm

On our way back to the ferry we thought we did not have enough time to do justice to Galicia and seeing as Amanda had not seen the Picos del Europa we decided to do these mountains properly in our last few days. We started in an area south of Bilbao where we visited some spectacular cascada through mountain villages and we worked our way Westwards through fantastic mountain ranges and parks to the Picos. This was the early morning view from our campsite perched up high on a lookout or mirador overlooking the village and valley of Portillo de Busto, looking towards Bilbao. We had a fabulous view of a Hobby as it flew past at dusk with prey probably a dragonfly.

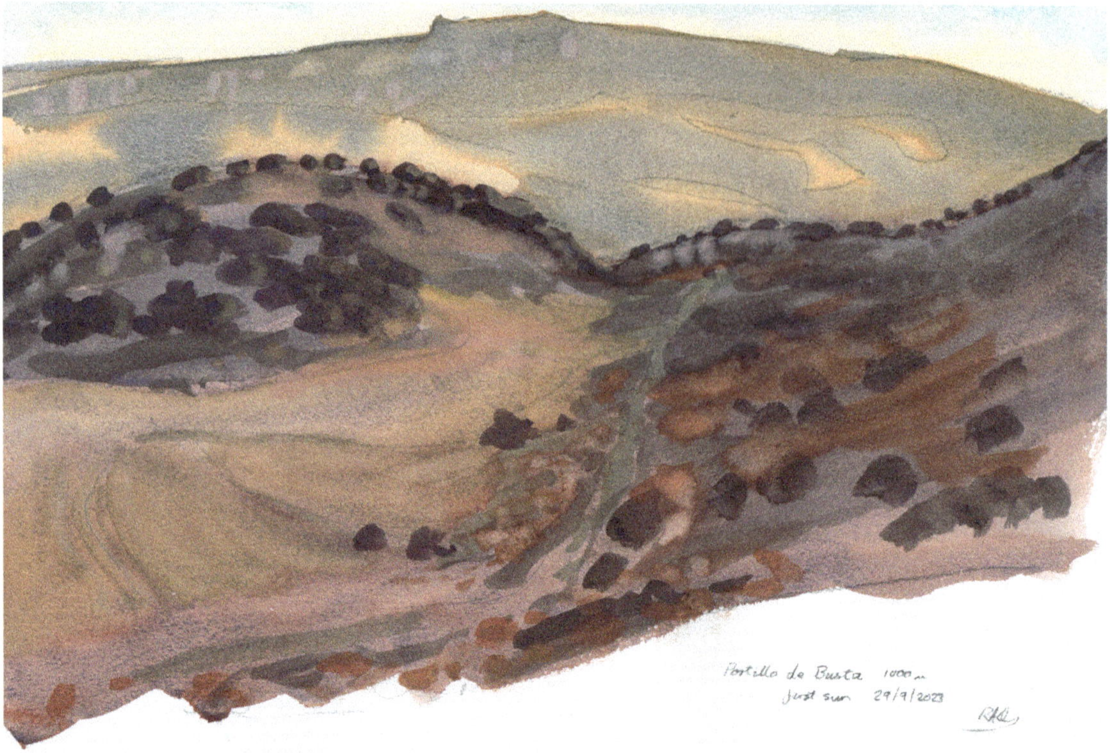

Portillo De Busto, first light

Watercolour on Fabriano 100% cotton cold-pressed
300gsm
unframed
45.5 x 35.5 cm

This is the first sun coming around the mountain to catch the tops of the oak trees as they lean out at all angles from the round rocky hillock and the glowing hillsides beyond. Plough-lines adding to the movement of the sweeping lands. It was almost eagle country but we didn't see any in these northern mountains until later in the day crossing West to the Picos into a more arid habitat, a magnificent pair of Golden Eagles hunting at altitude over a huge gorge.

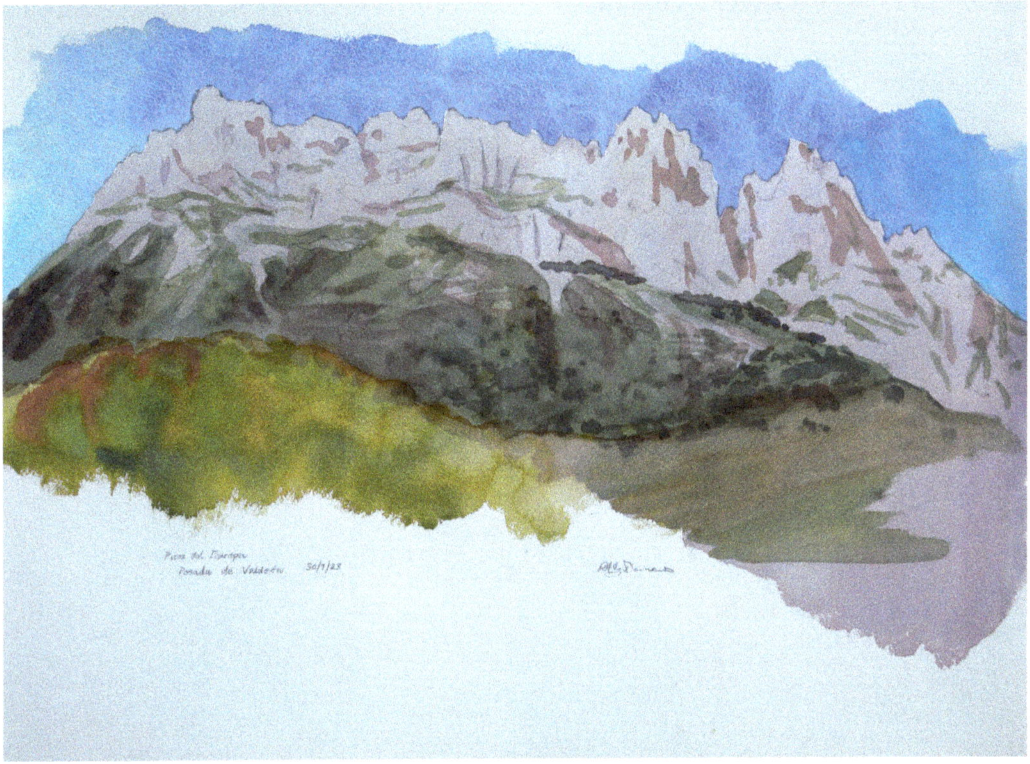

Picos de Europa, Posada de Valdeon

Watercolour on Arches Aquarelle Not 300gsm paper
unframed
77 x 57 cm

I just love the stark contrast of the white pinkish limestone peaks of the Picos against the fantastic deep blue sky. These are fairytale mountains very wild in their inaccessibility. A Buzzard was calling from the trees in the foreground. After the sketch we did a drive along the Cares Gorge as far as we could, which cuts through the wild heart of the Picos. It is renowned as one of the most dangerous roads! We camped in a really secluded spot. We saw plenty of Alpine Choughs, Ravens and Griffon Vultures around the cliffs and in the evening a Chamois appeared with its youngster.

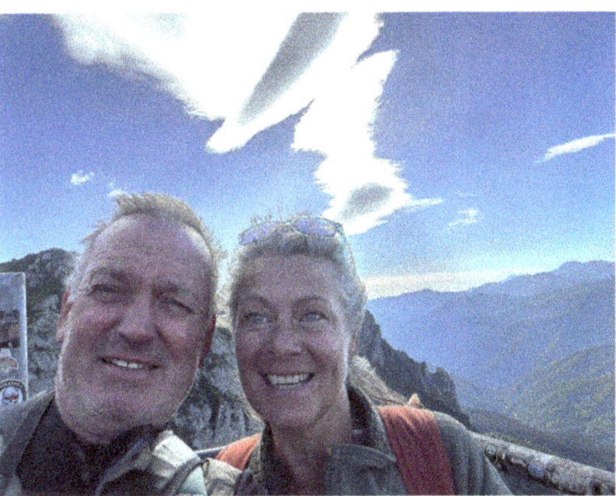

Nacreous (mother of pearl) clouds
at high altitude on the top of the Picos

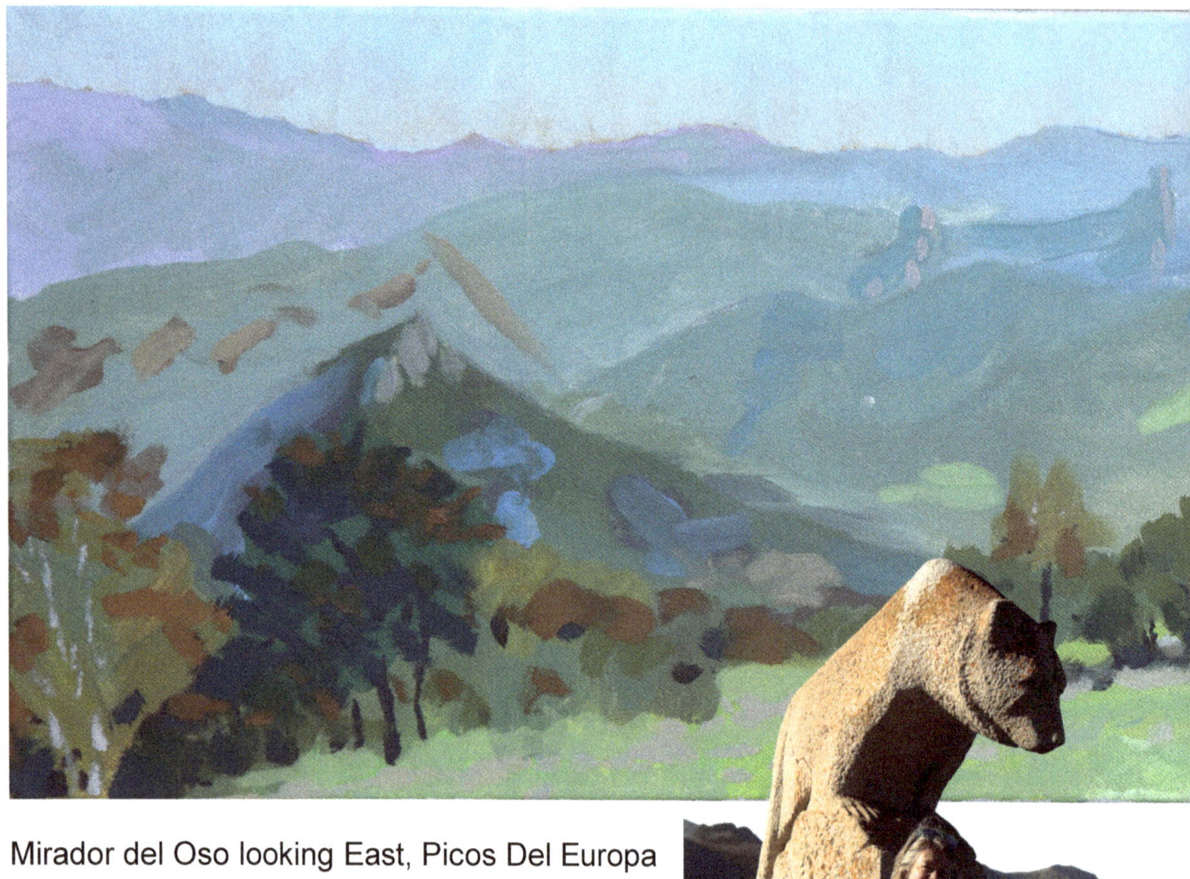

Mirador del Oso looking East, Picos Del Europa

Oil on canvas
unframed
100 x 30 cm

Amanda and the Bear

Just below the sculpture of the bear we found this fantastic view looking East across the Picos with the sun coming up beyond. Picos de Europa is an amazing mountain range rising to 2650m above sea level with the most dramatic bleached limestone peaks and pinnacles. We were at about 1600m but it was already hot (34 degrees) and we were surrounded by gentle cattle with bells ringing as they munched the grass almost between our feet. It was an idyllic scene. Beautiful rugged mountains that were home to the tough Celtic Cantabri who repelled the Romans. Now home to wolves and bears and other wild creatures. A bit further North from the Dehesa but on our way home and a great place to spend a few days.

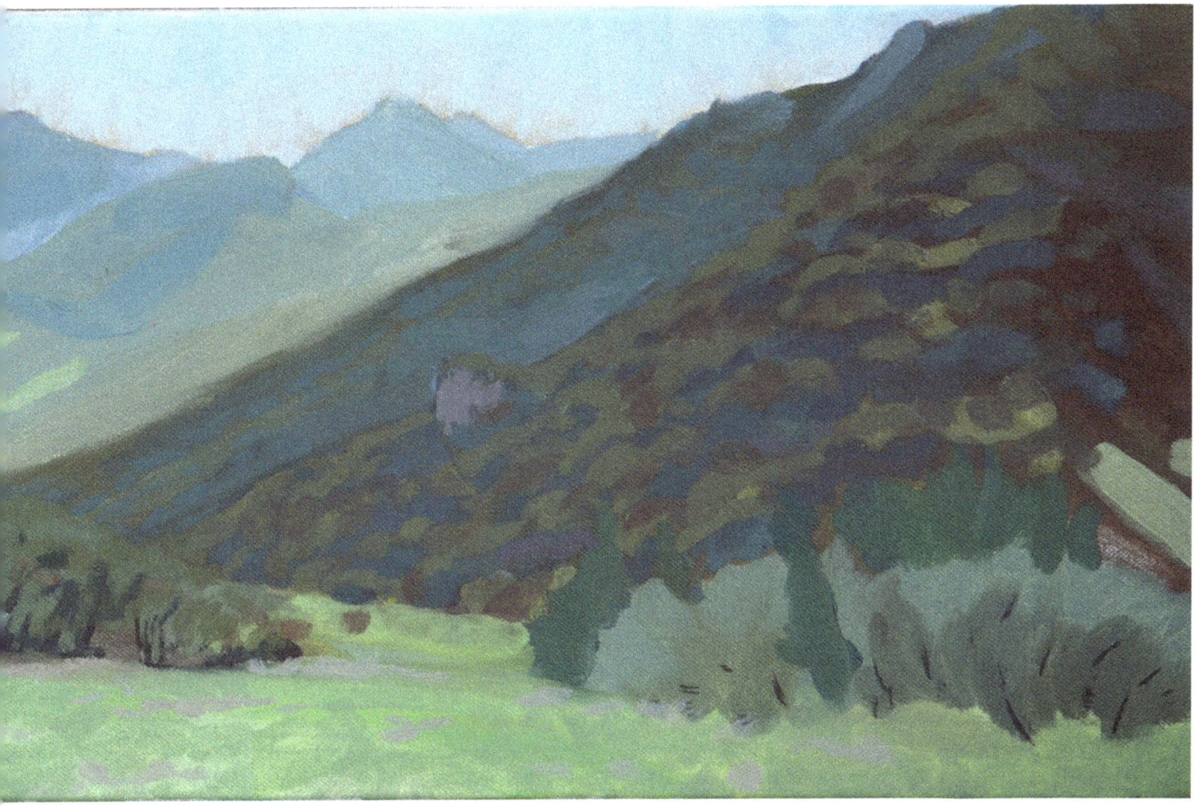

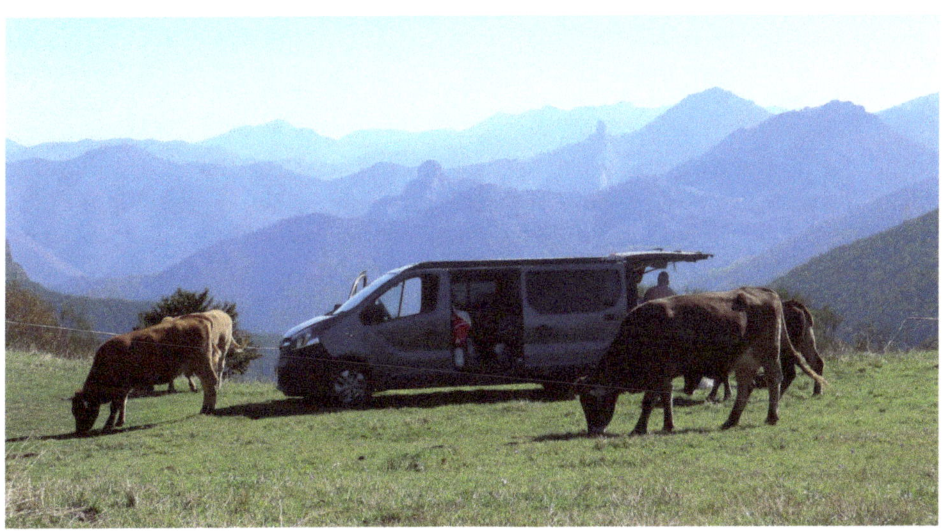

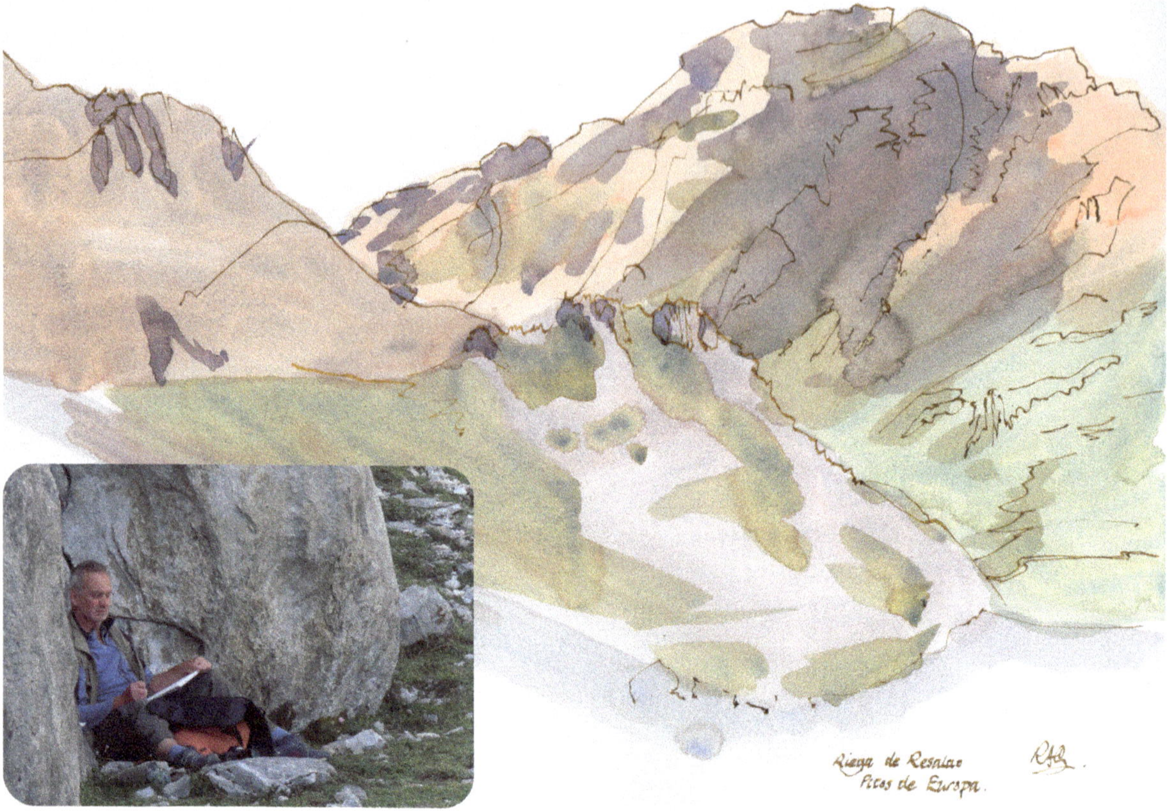

Riega de Resalao, Picos de Europa

Watercolour on Fabriano 100% cotton hot-pressed 300gsm
unframed
45.5 x 35.5 cm

We took the cable-car up the mountain to about 2400m from Fuente de Parador and did the same walk I did with Paddy and trekking team a decade before, up into the strange lunar landscape of the limestone Picos. Last time the weather had been outrageous with icy winds that made me realise how unprepared I had been, this time it was windy, not as cold, but with the most amazing jet-stream cloud formations overhead. After a hearty breakfast watching Alpine Choughs we headed up towards the 2600m peak and turned right exactly where we had last time to shelter under a rock outcrop on the steep scree from the piercing wind. This was the sketch in extreme conditions. Amanda a bit worried about our predicament but we made it back to the cable car and we didnt need to find refuge in the chalet cafe last time where I was introduced to the exceptionally reviving qualities of Pacharan! Fond memories set both times.

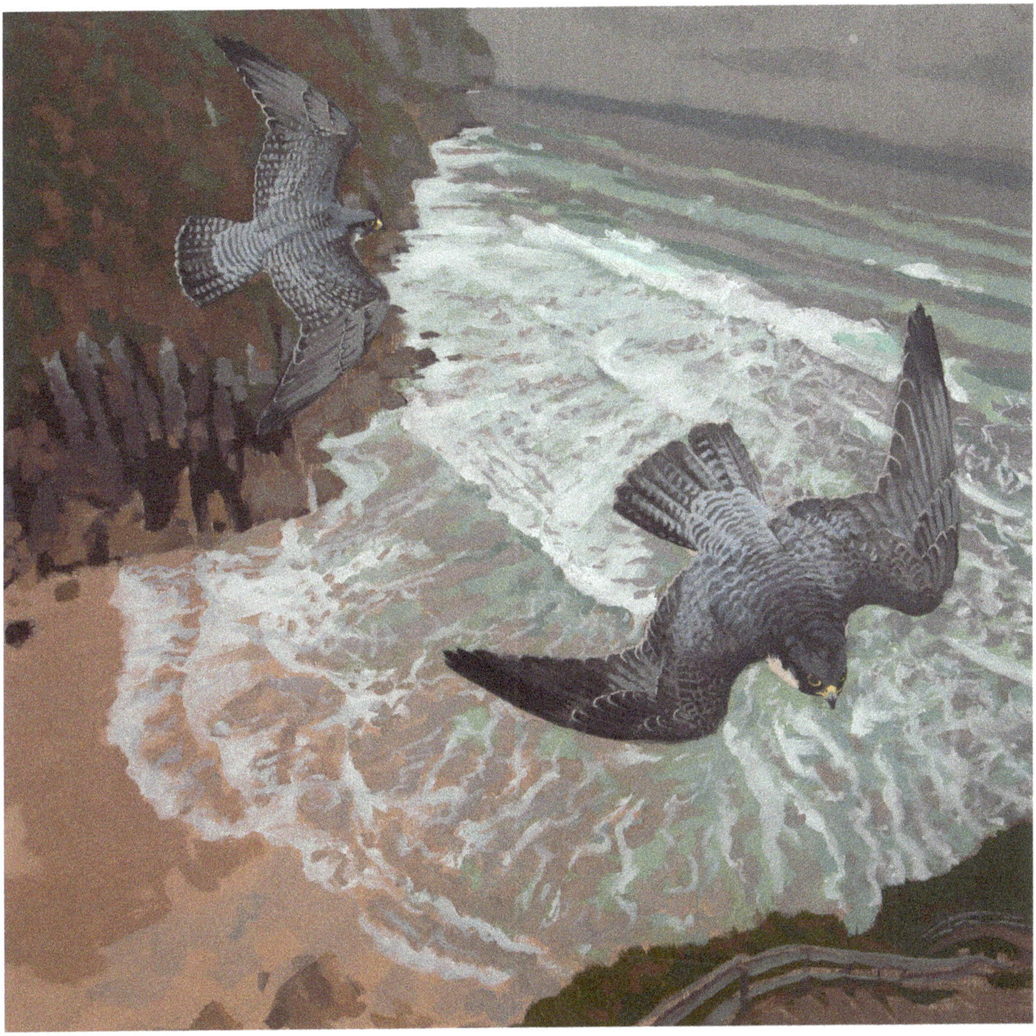

Peregrines at Punta de Vidiago

Oil on canvas
framed
60 X 60 cm

We stayed one of our last nights on the North Asturias coastline at a beautiful site recommended by Lulu and Simon. Paddy describes this coastline as very like Pembrokeshire which it us but the Atlantic Ocean here has deeper colours magnified somehow by the strong light and warm red sands. We watched a stunning pair of Peregrine Falcons flying together here, against the backdrop of Ensenada de Novales, towards Punta de Vidiago

Clark, W. & Davies, R. African Raptors. 2018. Helm Identification Guide. Bloomsbury Publishing Plc. London, Oxford, New York, New Delhi, Sydney. 336pp.

Aronson, J., Pereira, J.S. & Pausas, J.G. (Eds.) 2009. Cork Oak Woodlands on the Edge - Ecology, Adaptive Management and Restoration. Island Press. 315pp.

Markandya, A., Taylor, T., Longo, A., Murty, M.N., Murty, S. and Dhavala, K., 2008. Counting the cost of vulture decline—an appraisal of the human health and other benefits of vultures in India. Ecological economics, 67(2), pp.194-204.

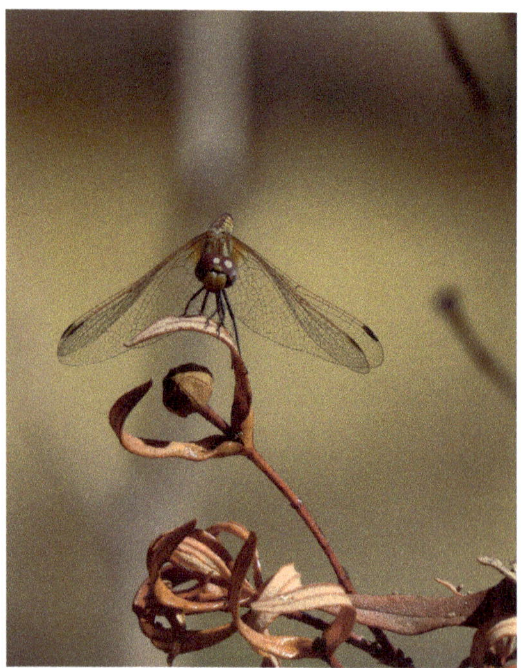

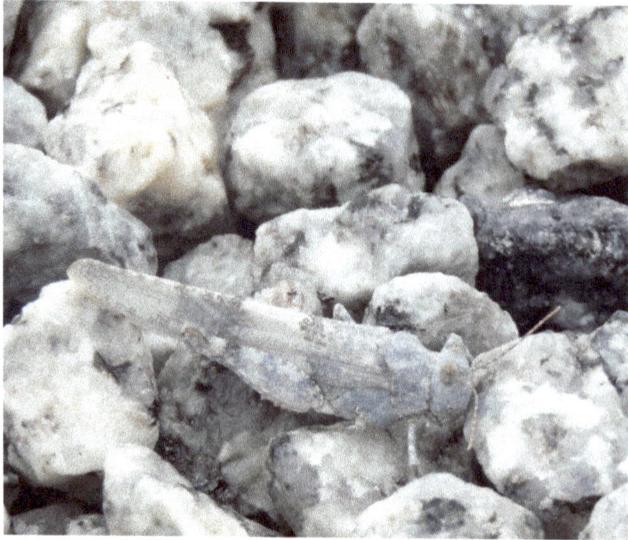

this grasshopper matched the stones perfectly, very similar to the pamphagid toadhoppers in the Karoo

TABLE OF OBSERVATIONS ON OUR JOURNEY

SPECIES	OBSERVATIONS	TOTAL SEEN
Griffon Vulture	120	931
Eurasian Buzzard	47	56
Black Kite	30	41
Eurasian Kestrel	18	24
Cinereous Vulture	11	20
Booted Eagle	13	17
Short-toed Snake-eagle	17	17
Unidentified Small Eagle	8	10
Western Marsh Harrier	9	10
Eurasian Sparrowhawk	6	6
Lesser Kestrel	2	6
Golden Eagle	3	5
Bonelli's Eagle	2	4
Peregrine Falcon (Brookei)	3	4
Red Kite	3	4
Egyptian Vulture	1	2
Spanish Imperial Eagle	2	2
Steppe Buzzard	2	2
Milvus Kite spp	1	1
Eurasian Hobby	1	1
Unidentified Buzzard	1	1
Unidentified Harrier	1	1
Unidentified Large Eagle	1	1
Western Honey-buzzard	1	1
White-tailed Sea-eagle	1	1

Plate 9 from African Raptors (Bloomsbury)
Griffon Vulture and Rueppell's Vulture

Watercolour & Gouache
on Waterstones hot-pressed 300gsm
framed
70 x 93 cm (frame)

This is the only painting not done as part of our Montado and Dehesa adventure. It is a large colour plate completed for a fieldguide on African Raptors that Rob did with American raptor expert, Bill Clark. But it features the Griffon Vultures (top half) which we saw so many of on our trip and it is still available to purchase as a framed original or as a print. Simply view the QR code above using your phone camera and navigate to the gallery website indicated. We will donate 25% of the net sale proceeds to Vulture Conservation Foundation.

The plate shows all identifiable sex and age classes in flight and perched as well as unusual colour morphs. Throughout the fieldguide Rob illustrated these birds against their favourite (and his favourite) habitats. The Griffon Vultures are shown against the view from Tarifa (a major migratory bottleneck for these birds to and fro Africa from Spain) across the straits of Gibraltar to the magnificent mountain, *Jebel Musa*, in Morocco. One of the pillars of Hercules, the name translates from Berber as Mount Moses.

The second species shown in the bottom half of the plate is the closely-related Rueppell's Vulture from the mountains of West and East Africa. All these large Gyps vultures do love magnificent mountains and the mountain shown behind these birds is called Ololokwe, a huge granite inselberg in the Samburu region of northern Kenya. Rob was actually directed there by his great friend Simon Thomsett, a raptor guru from these parts, who actually owns a time-share in a cave on the top of the mountain with a wild leopard (they share the accommodation quite amicably). On his first visit there Rob thought he was seeing swarms of swifts around the tops of the cliffs but the scalee of the rock is so vast it actually turned out to be swarms of Rueppell's Vultures. Let's do what we can to keep it that way..

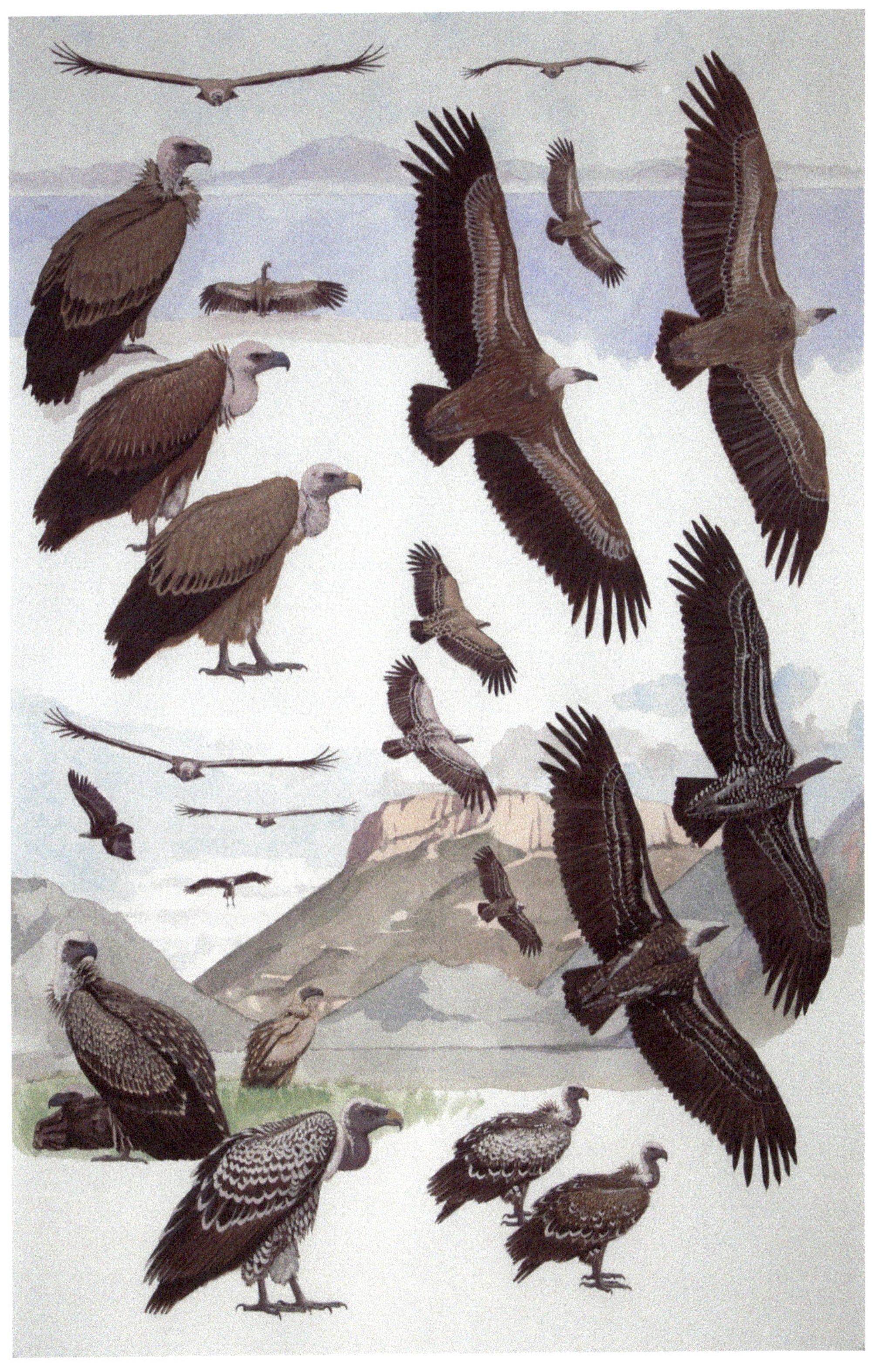

ABOUT THE AUTHORS

Amanda grew up in and around Oxfordshire, immersed in the great outdoors and nature. Now living in Pembrokeshire and, after taking a horticultural course at Pembrokeshire College, Amanda has built up her own successful gardening business. Her interests in plants, flowers and botanical diversity have expanded and this has encouraged Amanda to get back behind the camera.

Amanda's fascination for rural villages, waterfalls, landscapes and different cultures inspired her to take the plunge and travel around Portugal and Spain for five weeks in our trusty van, Myfanwy, capturing memorable images and enjoying a well-deserved break.

Amanda Squire

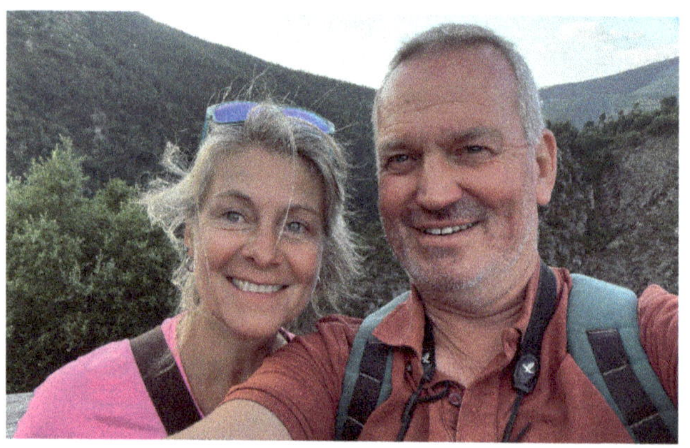

Dr Rob Davies

Rob studied zoology at Exeter University and worked as an ecologist / conservationist in Africa for 20 years. His early research studies led to a passion for a mapping technology called GIS which Rob has applied throughout his career to map protected areas, species distributions (notably birds of prey) and the harmful effects of climate change on African communities. After working closely with various NGOs in South Africa and UK this culminated in Rob setting up a consultancy called Habitat Info. Rob has kept his art going since school and he opened The Natural Gallery in 2019 to showcase his work alongside that of other artists with a similar passion for wildlife and nature. Over the years he has illustrated a monograph on the Black Eagle by Valerie Gargett and a fieldguide on African Raptors (Bloomsbury) with Bill Clark; and he is currently compiling work on the Karoo and the Pembrokeshire natural landscapes.

Together, Rob and Amanda have been carrying out a nature restoration project on the farm Llanunwas near Solva which links up wild habitats with neighbours The Bug Farm and local protected sites. The encouragement of wild meadow, wider hedgerows, pollinator plants in concert with arable fields is helping bring back species not seen locally for decades.

www.ingramcontent.com/pod-product-compliance
Lightning Source LLC
Chambersburg PA
CBHW042052030726
47599CB00019B/2463